# Entertaining Women

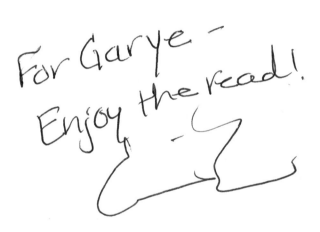

For Garye -
Enjoy the read!

# Entertaining Women:

*Actresses, Dancers, and Singers
in the Old West*

CHRIS ENSS

TWODOT®

GUILFORD, CONNECTICUT
HELENA, MONTANA

**A · TWODOT® · BOOK**

An imprint and registered trademark of Rowman & Littlefield

Distributed by NATIONAL BOOK NETWORK

British Library Cataloguing-in-Publication Information available

Library of Congress Cataloging-in-Publication Data available

ISBN 978-1-4422-4733-8 (paperback)
ISBN 978-1-4422-4734-5 (e-book)

♾™ The paper used in this publication meets the minimum requirements of American National Standard for Information Sciences—Permanence of Paper for Printed Library Materials, ANSI/NISO Z39.48-1992.

# Contents

# Acknowledgments

There are many people who helped in assembling material for this book, and I am indebted to them for their assistance. I wish to acknowledge with gratitude the fine staff at the California State Library for helping to gather information on many of the talented entertainers contained in this publication; the knowledge and indulgent personnel at the Searl's Library, the Doris Foley Library, and the Nevada County Historical Library; Mrs. Lee Cox at the San Francisco Performing Arts Library and Museum; the staff at the Indiana State Museum and the Allen County Public Library; the staff at the Rare Book and Manuscript Library at the University of Pennsylvania; the staff at the New York Public Library; Erin Chase at the Huntington Library; and Scott Gibson at Caxton Press.

A special thank you goes to talented Editorial Director Erin Turner, Digital and Social Media Marketing Manager Sarah Baker Givens, and Publicity Manager Sharon Kunz. Without their hard work and dedication this book would be little more than an idea.

# Introduction

In 1847 the western territory of the United States was a sleepy wilderness populated mostly by Indians and Mexicans. But when word reached the eastern states that there were rich deposits of gold in the mountains of the frontier, the region changed virtually overnight. Two hundred thousand restless souls, mostly men, but some women and children, traveled to the untamed western lands, primarily to California, during the first three years of the Gold Rush. They came from all over the world, leaving homes and families for the dream of finding riches.

Soon the West was dotted with mining boomtowns and bustling new cities. Fortunes were made and lost daily. Lawlessness was commonplace. At first, gold seekers were content with the crude entertainment provided by ragtag bands and their own amateur fiddle-playing neighbors. They flocked to bear-wrestling and prize-fighting exhibitions. In this impetuous atmosphere, gambling dens, saloons, brothels, and dance halls thrived, but after a while the miners and merchants began to long for more polished amusements.

Theaters, backstreet halls, tents, palladiums, auditoriums, and jewel-box-size playhouses went up quickly and stayed busy, their thin walls resounding with operas, arias, verses from Shakespeare, and minstrel tunes.

The western pioneers' passion for diversion lured brave actors, dancers, singers, and daredevils west. Entertainers endured the same primitive conditions as other newcomers. They lived in tents and deserted ship and canvas houses or paid enormous rents for the few available wooden cabins. But nineteenth-century thespians were often prepared for such a lifestyle. Acting was largely an itinerant profession at the time, and most players earned their living barnstorming from town to town, and even from country to country, performing different plays or musical numbers from a large repertoire every night of the week. Bored miners were willing to pay high sums to these entertainers, especially to the females.

Many of the most popular women entertainers of the mid- and late 1800s performed in the boomtowns that dotted the West, drawn by the same desire for riches and bringing a variety of talents and programs. They were mostly well received and sometimes literally showered with gold, but their personal lives were often marked by tragedy and unhappiness. Within the chapters of this book are the stories of a few of these gifted thespians who brought glitz, glamour, and genius to western America. The footlights have been illuminated, and the curtain is about to go up, revealing the tales of women entertainers who captured the hearts of the western pioneers.

# Catherine Norton Sinclair

## The Talented Divorcee

*You know as well as I do that the cause for my leaving you was the conviction of your infidelity.*

—EDWIN FORREST TO HIS WIFE, ACTRESS
CATHERINE NORTON SINCLAIR FORREST
SHORTLY AFTER HE DISCOVERED LOVE LETTERS
SHE HAD WRITTEN TO ANOTHER MAN.

Shakespearean actor Edwin Forrest rifled through the desk drawer in the sitting room of the New York home he shared with his wife, socialite-turned-actress-and-theater-manager Catherine Norton Sinclair. The contents of the drawer belonged to Catherine, but Edwin wasn't interested in maintaining her privacy. In his frantic search he uncovered a worn and rumpled letter written to his bride from fellow thespian George Jamieson. "And now, sweetest, our brief dream is over; and such a dream!" the correspondence began. "Have we not known real bliss? Have we not realized what poets have to set up as an ideal state, giving full license to their imagination, scarcely believing in its reality? Have we not experienced the truth that ecstasy is not fiction? And oh, what an additional delight to think, no, to know, that I have made some happy hours with you . . . With these considerations, dearest, our separation, though painful will not be unendurable; I am happy, and with you to remember and the blissful anticipation of seeing you again, shall remain so . . ." Jamieson's declaration of his feelings for Catherine ended with a promise to do "my utmost to be worthy of your love."

Edwin reread the letter with poised dignity, and on its completion he sank into the nearest chair, cursing the day he had met the woman he had married. After a few moments he arose and frantically paced about the room. He denounced Catherine for her infidelity and fell to the floor weeping uncontrollably. According to Edwin's biographer, William Rounseville Alger, Edwin was "struck to the heart with surprise, grief, and rage." Catherine's take on Edwin's reaction and the circumstances surrounding her husband reading the letter are vastly different from Alger's account. Almost from the moment the pair met, Edwin was jealous of everyone Catherine knew in her social standing and did not shy away from making a scene.

Catherine was born near London in 1818 to Scottish parents who had four children in all. Her father, John Sinclair, was a well-known vocalist who had toured America in 1831 and 1833. Historical records note that Catherine was endowed with natural beauty, and, whatever the quality and quantity of her formal and social education, she had in her teens acquired a sparkle and vivacity that attracted men. She was popular and well liked and attended formal soirees, theatre openings, and art exhibits with myriad friends from all walks of life.

In October 1836, Catherine and a gathering of women, who formed the social circle to which she belonged, attended a performance of a play called *The Gladiator*. The star of the show was Edwin Forrest. His talent on stage was exceptional, and he was quite aware of the genius he possessed. He relished the positive attention he received from critics and followers. He enjoyed giving spontaneous soliloquies to young women who approached him after a performance. When speaking in or about plays, particularly those of Shakespeare, Edwin exuded confidence. Off stage, however, he struggled to find his place. He was an uneducated man and self-conscious about his impoverished background and lack of refinement.

Catherine saw only an attractive, charismatic actor when they met after the play. The attention Edwin paid her when she met the rest of the cast flattered the young woman. The impressionable Catherine later wrote in her memoirs that "this is the handsomest man on whom my eyes have fallen." Edwin was taken with Catherine as well, but for different reasons. She was the daughter of a respectable genteel family of moderate means. Edwin believed Catherine would assure him an excellent social standing that would be beneficial for the advancement of his career.

Edwin and Catherine were wed on June 23, 1837, at St. Paul's Convent Garden in the city of London. The wedding was fashionable and showy, touched here and there by sophistication and culture. According to the August 19, 1837, edition of the *Boston Morning Post*:

> *The ceremony was performed by Reverend George Croly, in the presence of her father, who gave the bride away, and a long cortege of private friends of both parties.*
>
> *Upon leaving the church, Mr. Forrest led his young and lovely bride to a new and splendid carriage expressly manufactured for the occasion, and with the aid of four beautiful horses. The happy couple started for Windsor where it is their intention to pass a portion of their honeymoon.*
>
> *Miss Sinclair possesses a handsome fortune, which Mr. Forrest, much to his honor has settled on her, and the lady, upon her part, has been equally liberal, securing to him, in the event of her death, her property for life.*
>
> *The bride and bridegroom have postponed their departure from England until August 8. On the 18th of September, Mr. Forrest will reappear at the Park Theatre, New York, in the character of Othello.*
>
> *On the morning of his marriage, Mr. Forrest presented his friend, Mr. Jones, with a magnificent silver salver, upon which is neatly engraved the following inscription, "As a small, but sincere tribute of respect for him as a man, and as an acknowledgement of his friendly exer-*

Catherine Sinclair as Lady Teazle from the play *School for Scandal*

*tions, which overcame many objections, and prevailed on
me to appear on the British stage."*

In September the pair sailed to New York, where Edwin resumed his stage career. Catherine concentrated on making a home for her new husband and entertaining friends at the Forrests' elaborate town house on Twenty-Second Street. The friends she entertained had potential to benefit Edwin by investing in the various shows in which he starred.

According to the biography of Edwin's life penned in 1877, entitled *The Life of Edwin Forrest, the American Tragedian*, the marriage was doomed to fail because Edwin cared more about his work than his wife. "He was wholly engrossed in himself and neglected Catherine," Alger wrote. Rumors abounded that Edwin was also unfaithful. Catherine's friends resented how he treated her and refused to give him the proper consideration he felt he deserved.

By April 1, 1839, the award-winning tragedienne actor was aggravated with being married, and, according to the April 1, 1839, edition of the *Milwaukee Sentinel,* had petitioned for a divorce in a Philadelphia court. He cited the reason for the divorce as "infidelity"—not his own, but Catherine's. It was a claim her friends vehemently denied. Fearful that the public would side with his wife should he press the matter further, he withdrew his complaint and returned to Catherine, and the couple reconciled their differences.

The Forrests traveled from Massachusetts to Washington and then on to New Orleans as Edwin performed in theaters in those locations. Catherine learned a great deal about the art of acting while watching her accomplished husband. She also learned how to manage a theater by observing the experts at venues such as the National Theatre in Boston and the Bowery Theatre in New York.

In addition to acting, Edwin tried his hand at investing in stocks. The contacts he made through Catherine enabled him to gain inside knowledge of what companies to follow. Along with Horace Greeley, he was a majority stockholder in the Sylvania Association, which helped establish artists and playwrights by funding their early works, and later the talent would pay the company back with interest.

In 1845, the Forrests sailed to England where Edwin was to perform at the Princess Theatre in London. Catherine was eagerly welcomed home by her family and longtime friends. Edwin resented the attention paid to his wife and argued with her that he should have been the one given a hero's reception because he was a gifted and proven actor.

The Forrests returned to America in the summer of 1847, and their marriage limped along for another year after that. Adding more hurt to the problematic union was the death of the four children they had together. All died at birth. Distressed by their unsuccessful efforts to fulfill their domestic existence, they found companionship outside the home. Friends and relatives of both Edwin and Catherine weren't surprised to learn they had turned to others for affection; by all accounts the marriage had always been a disaster. Acquaintances reported that the source of the pair's problems was their vast difference in temperament. Catherine was sociable, and Edwin was private. Forrest's friend and author, James Reid, believed the couple's difficulties were a matter of "nationality." "If Mr. Forrest had established in his household certain rules," James wrote in his journal, "and taught his wife the difference between English and American habits, much of the evil arising out of their misunderstanding might have been obviated."

There was some truth to the assertion by Catherine's supporters that Edwin resented his wife's superior social position as much as he coveted it. Writing to his wife from Baltimore, for instance, he recounted that a "grand democratic procession" had passed in front of the theaters "with cheers for your humble servant. You will, I am sure, be gratified to hear this in spite of your pretended aristocracy."

The issue that prompted Edwin to again seek an official end to his marriage with Catherine occurred in the spring of 1848. The couple was in Cincinnati, Ohio, where Edwin was appearing in *King Lear*. During a break in rehearsals one afternoon, Edwin returned to his hotel room and found Catherine standing between the knees of George Jamieson. George's hands were resting on Catherine's waist. Edwin was furious. The two men scuffled, with Edwin getting the best of George. George fled the scene. Catherine tried to reason with Edwin, explaining that whatever happened between her and George should only be considered a "mere matter of indiscretion."

Shortly after the incident in Ohio, the Forrests had a serious argument about Catherine's parents. Edwin resented his in-laws and their friends. During the couple's heated exchange, Edwin made a derogatory accusation about Catherine's sister. Catherine called Edwin a liar. According to Alger, "The words 'It is a lie' fell into his irascible blood like drops of molten iron. He restrained his temper with great difficulty and stated, 'If a man had said that to me he should die, I cannot live with a woman who has said it.'"

Edwin escorted Catherine to the home of her friends, Parke and Fanny Goodwin, and left her there. Divorce was now inevitable. Catherine sent him several letters pleading to keep the demise of their marriage a secret from the press. Edwin initially agreed but decided against it when he learned the situation could be used to smear her name while bringing box office appeal to himself.

Edwin opened the doors to the home he had shared with Catherine and invited newspaper reporters and friends to come in and hear him talk of his woes. After announcing his marriage was over, he proceeded to explain in detail Catherine's many faults. When a listener attempted to defend her by praising her physical and spiritual beauty, Edwin replied, "She looks ugly to me. Her face is black and hideous."

The May 8, 1849, edition of the *Daily Banner* was one of many newspapers that printed articles about the Forrests' impending divorce. The report read,

> *The pair was living happily until the beginning of last winter, when Mr. Forrest became moody and melancholy.*
>
> *In the month of December, Mr. Forrest returned from a professional engagement in a most unhappy state of mind, and at once demanded a separation. He assigned no cause, offered no apology for the position he assumed; and when the immediate friends of the parties interfered, and asked to be informed why it was he asked for repudiation, his only reply was a studied, incomprehensible silence.*

Catherine's friends encouraged her to enter a countersuit in the divorce proceedings, charging Edwin with infidelity and extreme cruelty. She hired a prominent New York attorney named Charles O'Conner to represent her. He directed Catherine in every aspect of the trial, including what she wore to court. When the scandalous divorce hearing began in December 1851, Catherine's look made quite an impression on the press. A reporter from the *New York Herald* wrote, "Mrs. Forrest was habited in black, wore a black silk bonnet with a white cape and a black lace veil covering her face."

The courtroom was filled to overflowing with the city's most curious individuals. All wanted to get a glimpse of the "Feuding Forrests" and hear all the sordid details of what led to the downfall of the marriage. The *New York Times* covered the daily activities of the trial and the witnesses called to the stand and ran transcripts of what was said in the courtroom. A handful of people testified that they had seen Catherine behaving inappropriately with other men; one of those witnesses was Robert Garvin, a servant in the Forrests' home. He testified,

*I am a Protestant, Irishman from the North of Ireland, I came to this country in June 1848, or thereabouts and went to live with Mr. Forrest on 22nd Street in the city of New York, in the month of July of that year. I staid [sic] eight months with Mr. Forrest and left his service in March 1849; because the family was going to break up. During that time, up to the month of January 1849, or thereabouts, the conduct and demeanor of the said Edwin Forrest to his wife was always kind and affectionate.*

*Mr. Forrest was absent three times from the house while I was employed there, about two or three weeks, each time at least on professional business. When Mr. Forrest was at home the family was conducted in a very orderly manner, and the house was shut up generally about ten or eleven o'clock and I usually shut it up. When Mr. Forrest was absent, however, there were several gentlemen who were in the habit of staying very late. Mrs. Forrest would tell me, "I could go to bed," and after she and her visitors would sit up very late.*

*Some time in the course of the year a Mr. Richard Willis was secreted in the house for three days and three nights. One morning I saw him open the door to get fresh water, and in only his shirt and trowsers [sic]; the last of these nights there was a good deal of noise. Almost immediately after this, Mrs. Forrest and Mrs. N. P. Willis, Mrs. Woorhess, Richard Willis and Mr. Ibbotson sat up all night; I came down in the morning, and found them in the back drawing-room, in the same clothes they had on the night before; there were a few glasses lying about the table broken; they seemed to have been drinking a good deal.*

*After that, Mr. Richard Willis and Mrs. Forrest came home once very late, in a carriage together. She came home several times with drivers I had never seen before. When Mr. Forrest was at home she always went and came in another's carriage. On this occasion Mr. Forrest was absent. Mrs. Forrest got out of the carriage, and ran up the steps where I was standing. Mr. Willis put out his head and was getting out; when he saw me he went back into the carriage, but Mrs. Forrest called to him, "Richard, come on," and he followed her. Mrs. Forrest knew that I had seen him and that there was no use in trying to conceal it. Mr. Richard Willis never came when Mr. Forrest was at home.*

*After this, one day I let Captain Calcraft in, he went up into the library and Mrs. Forrest was there. Shortly after that, the same evening Mrs. Bedford went up and returned, and said she found the library door locked. My suspicions were excited, and I thought of climbing up the back piazza to look in through the window of the library, which was in the rear of the house; the blinds of the library window were shut tight, and I saw them shut the next day; the large library chair, which had a falling back, was found broken.*

*One night a man named Mr. Wyckoff brought home Mrs. Forrest from the theatre or opera in a carriage. I saw and heard them playing and skipping round in the lower hall, and to the best of my belief I heard him kiss her.*

Catherine's attorney denied Robert Gavin's testimony and called witnesses who reported a different version of Edwin's behavior. They testified to the outstanding character of his wife and the trauma she had endured in losing all of her children. Catherine's witnesses also testified that Forrest had not only formed many liaisons but had also been abusive in his treatment of Catherine and had driven her from their home.

Edwin lost his temper a number of times in court. He cursed and yelled at the judge and Catherine's lawyer whenever the subject of his infidelity was raised. Edwin was particularly enraged when the court was made aware of the affair he'd had with actress Josephine Cliften, a brawny, athletic woman with, in one reporter's account, "a bust finely developed, a physiognomy indicative of great firmness of character, and a mind rather of a masculine turn."

The Forrests' divorce case was played out in the public eye for a full six weeks. On January 25, 1852, the judge granted Catherine a decree of divorce. Edwin's behavior in court confirmed Catherine's claim of abuse, and she was granted the right to marry again when and if she chose. Forrest was denied that privilege and was ordered to pay all court expenses and three thousand dollars a year in alimony. According to the January 26, 1852, edition of the *New York Daily Times*, "Mrs. Forrest was thoroughly vindicated by the court, possessed public sympathy, and had before her a prospect of a quiet social life, with an income of money and of the world's esteem that will secure for her a select association of vulnerable friendship." Edwin was appalled by the decision and vowed to appeal the court's ruling.

With the divorce behind her, Catherine turned her full attention toward finding work. She decided to pursue a career in the field where she'd gained the most experience in the last ten to twelve years, the theater. She briefly studied acting with popular British thespian George Vandenhoff. Catherine Sinclair made her stage debut on February 2, 1852, in the play *The School for Scandal* at the Brougham's Lyceum Theatre in New York. She drew a large crowd of curious people to the first performance. They left excited about what they had seen Catherine do onstage and shared their opinion with others who swarmed to the theater to see the show for themselves. Audiences and critics were complimentary of her performance as Lady Teazle.

Catherine followed her performance in *The School for Scandal* with leading roles in *Lady of Lyons*, *Much Ado About Nothing*, *Love's Sacrifice*, and the *Patrician's Daughter*. Although she was "consistent and entertaining" in the plays in which she was featured, attendance fell with each production. People were not as interested in the socialite-turned-actress as they had been immediately after the divorce. Catherine was well aware that she was no longer a moneymaker for the theater companies. At the conclusion of the theatrical season in June 1852, Catherine left New York and traveled to England to see her family. She had hoped to invade the English theater while visiting London, but she was unable to secure an engagement because of the unfavorable publicity surrounding her due to the divorce.

Not one to be left idle, Catherine decided to try her hand at writing. The reviews of the novels she wrote, entitled *Beatrice*,

*Modern Accomplishment*, and *Lord of Lady Harcourt*, were favorable. "*Beatrice* is written with great care and tenderness," one critic noted in the November 13, 1852, edition of the *London Standard*. "In scenes of description or emotion Miss Sinclair has taken a step forward and exhibited a spirit which we have not recognized before." Another review wrote, "We feel no hesitation in predicting for this new production of Miss Catherine Sinclair eager readers and a great run."

In 1853 Catherine returned to America and joined an acting troupe touring the United States. Several towns denied the troupe admission on the grounds that the public was not interested in dramatic entertainment nor would they take into their midst a notorious woman, a female who dared violate her marriage vows. Catherine's most enthusiastic audience was in New Orleans. Theatergoers were thrilled to see her and cheered her each night she performed.

On May 5, 1853, Catherine arrived in San Francisco. Residents of the city welcomed her with open arms. The May 6, 1853, edition of the *Daily Alta California* announced her landing via the steamer the *Panama*:

> *Mrs. Sinclair has met with much success in Atlantic cities and previous to her departure for this country, concluded a long and successful engagement in New Orleans; embarking from that port for this 'land of promise,' as she pictures it. We certainly hope it may prove to Mrs. S. a land of abundant realizations. It is the intention of Mrs. S., we believe, to make her debut in one of her favorite pieces at the San Francisco Theatre. We predict crowded houses. Though she has come among us unannounced, she is not unknown, nor will she fail to meet all the sympathy and encouragement as a woman and as an artist that her talents and position entitled her to an intelligent and generous community.*

Throughout the summer of 1853, Catherine played several engagements in San Francisco, Sacramento, and Marysville. Not all the reviews of her work were necessarily glowing. According to an article in the July 24, 1853, edition of *Golden Era* newspaper, "Mrs. Sinclair's performances have improved materially since her first engagement in this city. Her acting is by no means faultless," the article noted. "It must be acknowledged that as a tragedienne, she has no rival in California." Despite her critics, she made numerous friends who thought everything she did onstage was outstanding. She gained ground both socially and professionally. In August 1853 the gentlemen composing the First California Battalion gave her a complimentary benefit. The event was significant because it was the first of its nature to be given to an artist in California.

By November 1853 Catherine had decided to combine her acting skills with managing a production and the new theater where the production would debut. The magnificent Metropolitan Theatre opened its door on December 24, 1853, presenting *The School for Scandal* with Catherine Sinclair as Lady Teazle and distinguished actor James E. Murdoch as her leading man. Matilda Heron and Edwin Booth (brother to John Wilkes Booth, who later assassinated Abraham Lincoln), stars in their own rights, were among the cast, too. A report in the January 1, 1854, edition of the *Golden Era* newspaper proclaimed Catherine to be "an exceptional woman who has reached the height of her career. She has found her niche in her chosen profession as manager."

Catherine managed the Metropolitan Theatre from November 1853 to March 1856. In addition to directing the behind-the-scenes activities at the Metropolitan Theatre, she also took a turn at managing the American Theatre in Sacramento. Ernest Harold, a pioneer actor, attributed her success as a manager to "extravagant spending." Ernest shared with reporters at the *Golden Era* newspaper:

> *The salaries she paid at the Metropolitan were unprecedented. She was a lady of profuse liberality, generous*

*impulses, brilliant accomplishments, and a supremely finished education. Mrs. Sinclair's prodigality was in the lavish expenditure of money in the production of plays and operas, and engaging the very artists at enormous expense, employing permanently a dramatic corps, opera company, and ballet troupe.*

On April 26, 1856, Catherine left San Francisco for Australia. After a short time there, performing with a troupe of actors who had appeared at the Metropolitan Theatre during her time managing the business, she traveled to England to visit her ailing father. Catherine returned to the London stage in November 1857, playing Beatrice in Shakespeare's comedy *Much Ado About Nothing*. The notices published in the London papers reported that she was a "most decided success." The November 5, 1857, edition of the *Daily Alta California* relayed the opinion of the English audience. The article read,

*Her talents were made evident in the first scene. Her conception of the part of Beatrice is distinguished by sound judgment and excellent taste. Her animal spirits are very great, and she never loses a chance of making a point. In everything she does she indicates the careful, studious, and conscientious artist. The audience received her with unusual marks of distinction throughout the performance and recalled her at the end of the third act and the fall of the curtain.*

Catherine returned to America in December 1858. She planned to make a starring tour through the country with her fiancé, musical composer George Loder. Edwin Forrest had no intentions of allowing his ex-wife to marry another man and live happily ever after. Since the Forrests' divorce had become final in 1852, Edwin had continued to pursue a way to prove Catherine had been guilty of adultery. He was still battling with the courts when Catherine's engagement was announced. Edwin could not persuade a judge to see things his way, and, in early 1859, his case was dismissed and one thousand dollars more was added to the alimony he was to continue paying Catherine. Ultimately she and George called off their wedding and went their separate ways. Edwin continued to seek out a court that would act on his behalf.

Catherine Norton Sinclair retired from the stage in late 1859. Her final performance was on December 18, 1859, at the Academy of Music in New York. She lived a fairly secluded life with her sister, Mrs. Henry Sidley, at the actress-manager's home in Staten Island. Occasionally a newspaper article about the accomplished theater manager would appear, explaining to readers how she was spending her remaining days in peace. The April 4, 1889, edition of the *Hawarden Independent* read,

> *Very few people outside her own family and immediate circle are aware of the fact that the lady is still alive and a resident of this city. And yet the tottering, white-haired, venerable looking matron, who every fine sunshiny morning about eleven o'clock is tenderly assisted down the steps of a residence on West 84th Street, and tucked away under heavy fur robes in a carriage, was forty years ago the bride of the great tragedian, the joy of his life and the sharer of his triumphs. She has passed by nearly three years the span of life allotted to man by the prophet, but although her frame is feeble and her eyes dim, her memory is clear and vigorous and she is never so happy as when recalling her childhood days and never so sad as when recalling her life with Edwin Forrest and the litigation that came as a result of their troubled marriage.*

Edwin finally abandoned the court battle against his ex-wife in 1868. He died four years later on December 12, 1872. According to the December 19, 1872, edition of the *Indiana Democrat*, Edwin was found lying dead on his bed by his housekeeper. The December 13, 1872, edition of the *Fort Wayne Daily Sentinel* announced the actor's passing and expanded on his long, illustrious career in the theater. "Personally, Mr. Forrest was not popular," the article read. "He was overbearing in demeanor and morose in disposition. He formed few friendships and made many enemies, both among his fellow actors and his social acquaintances. His treatment of his wife, a most estimable lady, did much to estrange the few friends he had."

Catherine passed away on June 16, 1891. Broken in health, she had gone blind in 1881. She lived out her last days with her nephew. Theater historians recognize Catherine as the most dynamic force in the national world of theater in the 1850s. She was seventy-four when she died and is buried at the Silver Mount Cemetery in Staten Island.

# Adah Menken

## The Frenzy of Frisco

*A striking picture, it was far out of the common run in that day:
a head of Byronic mold; a fair, proud throat, quite open to admiration, for the sailor collar that might have graced the wardrobe
of the Poet-Lord was carelessly knotted upon the bosom with a
voluminously flowing silk tie. The hair, black, glossy, short and
curly, gave to the head, forehead and nape of the neck a half-
feminine masculinity suggestive of the Apollo Belvedere.*

—Poet Charles Warren Stoddard's description of Adah Menken's portrait on
display at San Francisco's Maguire Opera
House in July 1863.

On August 24, 1863, San Francisco's elite flocked to Maguire's
Opera House. Ladies in diamonds and furs arrived in handsome carriages; gentlemen in opera capes and silk hats strutted in
stylishly. It was an opening night such as the city had never before
seen. All one thousand seats in the theater were filled with curious spectators anxious to see the celebrated, melodramatic actress
Adah Menken perform.

Adah was starring in the role that made her famous, that of
Prince Ivan in *Mazeppa*. It was rumored that she preferred to play
the part in the nude. Newspapers in the East reported that audiences found the scantily clad thespian's act "shocking, scandalous,
horrifying and even delightful." The story line of the play was
taken from a Byron poem in which a Tartar prince is condemned
to ride forever in the desert stripped naked and lashed to a fiery,

untamed steed. Adah insisted on playing the part as true to life as possible.

The audience waited with bated breath for Adah to walk out onto the stage, and, when she did, a hush fell over the crowd. She was beautiful, possessing curly dark hair and big dark eyes. Adorned in a flesh-colored body nylon and tight-fitting underwear, she left the audience speechless. During the play's climatic scene, supporting characters strapped the star to the back of a black stallion. The horse raced up the narrow runway between cardboard mountain crags. The audience responded with thunderous applause. Adah Menken had captured the heart of another city in the West.

Adah Isaacs Menken was born Adois Dolores McCord on June 15, 1835, in New Orleans, Louisiana. Her mother was a very beautiful French Creole, and her father was a highly respected free Negro. Prejudice against her ethnicity plagued her early career. Theater owners who were familiar with her heritage refused to hire her. As a result Adah created many stories about her upbringing and parentage. Historians believe this was necessary for her to secure work and be accepted by audiences across the United States. The confusion about Adah's lineage added a hint of mystery to her image. The truth about her roots was not uncovered until the early 1900s.

Adah's father died when she was seven. A few years after his death, her mother married Dr. J. C. Campbell, the chief surgeon of the US Army. According to biographies about Adah's life, Campbell was a generous man who encouraged the talents of Adah and her sister. Adah was a gifted writer, painter, actress, and dancer. By the time she was eleven, she was an accomplished artist, having published several poems and danced in the ballet of the French Opera House in New Orleans. She was exceedingly bright and fluently spoke French, Spanish, and Hebrew.

At thirteen Adah was crushed when her stepfather died, because she had come to count on his encouragement and support

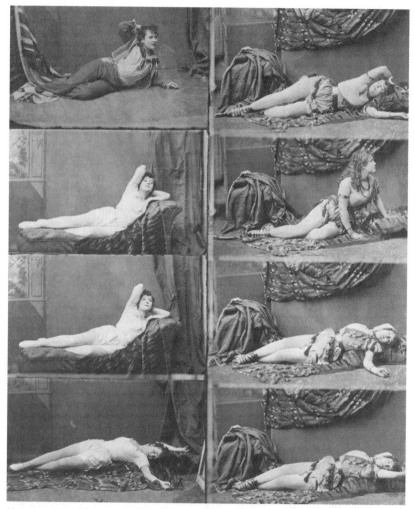

Known as the "Frenzy of Frisco" Adah Menken posed in eight seductive pictures that circulated throughout the West during the height of her acting career.
COURTESY OF THE LIBRARY OF CONGRESS

in her acting aspirations. Adah's relationship with her mother was strained. She was jealous of the affection her husband showed for Adah and thus treated her badly. In a letter to her sister dated July 1867, Adah wrote about how her mother "disliked her" and how she dreamed of a better life.

Shortly after Dr. Campbell's death, Adah's mother took up company with a man who made improper advances toward her daughters. Adah left home when she could suffer it no longer. She joined a local troupe of entertainers and traveled to Havana, Cuba, to dance for political figures and foreign dignitaries. She was well received and called the "Queen of the Plaza." A fellow actor named Horace Keene, who was on tour with Adah at this time, wrote, "Scarcely 16 [sic], she overwhelmed the audience with her charm and talent. Her tiny frame, crisp black curls and dark, sparkling eyes made her a beauty unlike any that have entertained here before. Is it any wonder Havana is bewitched by her?"

All the applause and attention she received helped Adah forget her sorrow over the loss of her stepfather. The players in her troupe convinced her she could earn more money as an actress than as a dancer. When she returned to the United States, she abandoned ballet and turned to acting.

The young girl began her quest for stardom in Liberty, Texas. She made a living giving public readings of Shakespeare's works, writing newspaper articles and poems, and teaching dance classes. She began to search for a rich husband to support her acting career by placing an advertisement in the *Liberty Gazette* newspaper on November 23, 1855: "I'm young and free, the pride of girls with hazel eyes and nut brown curls. They say I'm not void of beauty—I love my friends and respect my duty. I've had full many a BEAU IDEAL, yet never, never found one real. There must be one I know somewhere, in all this circumambient air; And I should dearly love to see him! Now what if you should chance to be him?"

Alexander Isaacs Menken, a well-to-do pit musician and conductor, was touring the Texas Panhandle when he came upon Adah's delightful poem. He wrote to her, and the two met, instantly firing one another with passion and ambition. They were married the following April in Galveston, Texas. Soon after Adah and Alexander said "I do," Adah began working onstage in supporting roles at the Liberty Shakespeare Theater and, with her husband's financial help, quickly moved on to lead roles at the Crescent Dramatic Association of New Orleans.

Alexander worshiped his new bride, and Adah was quite taken with him, but their notions of what married life should be were diametrically opposed. Alexander wanted a traditional, stay-at-home wife who would make his meals and raise his children. Adah was not at all interested in such a domestic life; in fact in one of the articles she wrote for the *Liberty Gazette*, she said that "women should believe there are other missions in the world for them besides that of wife and mother." The only beliefs Adah shared with Alexander were his religious ones. She adopted his Jewish faith and remained steadfast in it until her death.

Regardless of his opinions, Alexander found himself relying on the money Adah was making when he lost his fortune in ill-advised real estate investments. Adah tried to bolster his demoralized spirit by naming him her manager, but new marital troubles were on the horizon. Adah enjoyed the adulation of her audiences and the adoration of the young men who gathered at the stage door, roses in their arms. Alexander was extremely jealous of the attention she was given. He distanced himself from his popular, independent wife when she insisted on wearing pants and smoking in public, things proper women of the time absolutely did not do. When he could tolerate it no more, the pair separated.

Adah got over the collapse of her marriage by going on another acting tour. She traveled across the Great Plains and the West, performing in the plays *Great Expectations* and *Mazeppa*.

Dressed in risqué costumes, the immodest Adah packed houses in boomtown theaters, prompting overeager critics to state, "Prudery is obsolete now." Frontier men fell in love with Adah's style, lovely face, and exquisite figure.

Adah was one of the first actresses to recognize the value of photography for both publicity and posterity. Playbills featuring her picture preceded her arrival, appearing in every newspaper and on every theater anywhere near where she was set to perform. Her portrayal of the Prince of Tartar in *Mazeppa* and a lovesick sailor boy in the play *Black-Eyed Susan* brought rave reviews from theater critics everywhere. One critic was so impressed with her daring ability to take on men's roles that he proclaimed her to be "the finest actress in the country." Victor Hippard of the *New York Sentinel Critic* wrote, "She glosses my face with laughter and tears. She is the Aphrodite the male world has waited for . . . she is a rare beauty perched upon one of Heaven's high hills of light."

When Adah wasn't acting, she was honing her writing skills, penning poems for a new book, and contributing articles to a publication called *Israelite*. In these articles she called upon the Jewish people to defend themselves against injustices and prepare for the return to Zion. Her essay on Jews in Parliament that appeared in the September 3, 1858, issue was a powerful plea for the right of Jewish men to sit in the British House of Parliament as elected members. Scholars took notice of her work and often used quotes from her articles in their lectures. As pleased as she was to be taken seriously as a writer and an actress, a whirlwind affair with prizefighter John "Benicia Boy" Heenan convinced her to abandon her talents for a time to concentrate on being a wife and mother.

John was a six-foot, two-inch Irishman who met Adah backstage after one of her performances at the National Theater in Cincinnati. His fame as a pugilist had traveled ahead of him, and Adah was fascinated. John proposed, asking her to retire from her professions and concentrate solely on their marriage. Remarkably, she agreed and married John on September 3, 1859. On their honeymoon John taught her how to box; she soon learned to hold her own and would spar with him good-humoredly. After a month of marriage, the good humor was lost when John started beating Adah every night after dinner.

Like Alexander, John was jealous of the attention his wife received from her admiring fans. He felt threatened by the fact that his wife earned more money for her work than he did. Their stormy marriage came to an abrupt end when Alexander turned up and announced that he had never secured a divorce from Adah. The enraged boxer sailed to London to fight in the World Heavyweight Championship, leaving Adah to face the scandal alone. Alexander officially divorced Adah, and, even though she was three months pregnant with John's child, Adah divorced John soon after. It was a difficult pregnancy. Adah was able to carry the baby to term and give birth to a son, but he died a few hours later.

By August 1860, Adah Menken was at the lowest point of her life and career. The *New York Sunday Mercury* published copies of her poems of despair. Critics considered her poems to be "more self-revealing than those which any other female American poet had ever dared to publish." After a long period of sorrow, Adah decided to return to the stage. She vowed to "assault the highest citadels of the theater" and to "never again be a victim or sacrifice anything for the male-dominated society." She had no idea how soon she'd be put to the test.

Adah played theaters throughout the country in lead roles in *The Soldier's Daughter* and *The French Spy*. Audiences still went wild for her. Critics called her a second Lola Montez, comparing her to the Gold Rush performer known for being bawdy and without inhibitions, and observed that "her style of acting is as free from the platitude of the stage as her poetry is from the language." Her poems and articles were distributed freely to be reprinted in

Adah Menken

the newspapers of the towns in which she performed. Her plays drew expectant crowds all across the country.

About this time Adah fell in love again, this time with Robert Henry Newell, the literary editor of the *New York Sunday Mercury*. After reading her poetry and watching her performances, he was convinced they were destined to be together. He thought she had the "keenest mind" he had "ever encountered in a member of her sex." Adah felt the intellectual Robert would make a fine husband, and so the two were married on September 24, 1862. During their honeymoon Robert's true intent for his wife was revealed. He insisted that she give up her career and make serving him her life's work, informing her that she could read and write only poetry in her spare time. The bride made a hasty escape.

The brief marriage was sniggered over in the press. Adah publicly acknowledged that she was not very good at choosing leading men for her own life. "Being a wife was never my most successful performance," she admitted. Her failed marriages gave her an even more liberated view of the role of women. "A man discovered America," she wrote, "but a woman equipped the voyage. So everywhere; man executes the performance, but woman trains the man. Every effectual person, leaving an impress on the world is but another Columbus, whose mind was trained and furnished by some Isabella, in the form of his Mother, Wife, or Sister. Will men never learn to be grateful?"

Adah returned to California, wanting to distance herself from bad press and the growing conflict in the East that would lead to the Civil War. Newspapers throughout Gold Country happily reported she was booked for a one-hundred-night engagement at Maguire's Opera House in San Francisco.

Tom Maguire, an important player in San Francisco's theatrical scene, was thrilled that Adah had agreed to perform at his establishment. He gave her the greatest publicity campaign ever devoted to a theatrical event in San Francisco. Before opening night the entire run was sold out. San Franciscans didn't care about her reputation; they just wanted to see her for themselves.

Although Adah's form-fitting costumes were the most risqué anyone had seen onstage since Lola Montez, Tom was not entirely satisfied and asked Adah to remove even more clothing for the benefit of the males in the audience. After a considerable increase in her salary, Adah agreed to wear only a simple blouse and a pair of shorts that revealed most of her legs. The costume was scandalous for the time and shocked the public so much that people literally fought for the privilege of seeing the "naked lady." Adah performed many roles, but no matter the part, in the last scene she'd strip down to almost nothing.

Members of an organization called the Reform Group complained that "her style belonged more to the wild old time of the Forty-Niners, than to a respectable society where many days often pass without any murders at all." Nonetheless, her unique style made her a rich woman, and she wasn't about to censor her act. Adah Menken's amazing success in California theatrical history wasn't matched until films became popular.

As her fame increased, Adah gained and lost two more husbands and had another child. She never stopped working, though, and became known as the "Frenzy of Frisco." San Francisco adopted her as its favorite daughter. The Saint Francis Hook and Ladder Company made her an honorary member of its firefighting brigade; she was presented with a beautiful belt, and the entire brigade, including a brass band, serenaded her.

Journalists, too, were happy with her cultivated eccentricities, and they devoted many lines of text to her. Although the Civil War was raging back east and California was pro-Union, Adah spread a large Confederate flag across one wall of her hotel room. By day she walked the streets clad only in a single yellow silk garment. "Yellow," she said, was "her mystical color," and when writer Joaquin Miller called upon her for an interview, he found her lying upon a yellow rug, clothed in a yellow sheath. He was transfixed by the costume and wrote, "I doubt if any other woman in the world could wear a dress like that in the winds of San Francisco and not look ridiculous."

Adah wasn't satisfied with being only the "Frenzy of Frisco." She wanted to be the frenzy of the entire West. In 1864 she took to the road again, traveling east to Virginia City, Nevada. The *Gold Hill News* touted the actress' arrival on the front page:

> *She has come! The Menken was aboard one of the Pioneer coaches which reached Gold Hill this morning, at half-past eleven o'clock. She is decidedly a pretty little woman, and judging her style we supposed she does not care how she rides—she was on the front seats with her back turned to the horses. She will doubtless draw large houses in Virginia City, with her Mazeppa and French Spy in which she excels any living actresses.*

Adah opened her Virginia City show on March 2, 1864. Tickets ranged in price from one dollar for a single seat to ten dollars for a private box. The theater was packed on opening night. Many people were forced to stand in the aisles, and hundreds were turned away. Local critics, including a young Samuel Clemens (later to be known as Mark Twain), were present to review her performance. Adah was ushered onto the stage by thunderous applause. She brought down the house, and appreciative miners threw silver ingots at her feet. Sam Clemens was thoroughly impressed. His description of her performance published in the *Humboldt Register* is considered the best surviving account of Adah in action:

> *I went to see her play Mazeppa, of course. They said she was dressed from head to foot in flesh-colored "tights," but I had no opera-glass, and couldn't see it, to use the language of the inelegant rabble. She appeared to me to have but one garment on—a thin tight white linen one, of unimportant dimensions; I forget the name of the articles, but it is in-*

*dispensable to infants of tender age—I suppose any young mother can tell you what it is, if you have the moral courage to ask the question. With exception of this superfluous rag, the Menken dresses like the Greek Slave; but some of her postures are not so modest as the suggestive attitude of the latter. She is a finely formed woman down to her knees. . . .*

*Here every tongue sings the praises of her matchless grace, her supple gestures, her charming attitudes. Well, possibly, these tongues are right. In the first act she rushes out on stage, cavorting around; she bends herself back like a bow; she pitches headforemost at the atmosphere like a battering ram; she works her arms, and her legs, and her whole body like a dancing jack; her every movement is as quick as thought. . . . If this be grace then the Menken is eminently graceful.*

Adah earned an estimated $150,000 from her twenty-nine Nevada shows. When it came time for her to leave Virginia City, lovesick miners presented her with a silver brick valued at $403.31. It was stamped: MISS ADAH ISAACS MENKEN FROM FRIENDS OF VIRGINIA CITY, NEVADA TERRITORY—MARCH 30TH, 1864. Their devotion to the actress didn't end there—they named a local mine after her and formed the Menken Shaft and Tunnel Company. The company's stock certificates bore a picture of a naked lady bound to a galloping stallion. Adah left Nevada promising she'd return as soon as she could.

She traveled to Europe, still performing in *Mazeppa*, and toured Paris and Vienna. Although her talent was appreciated abroad, she never felt more loved or accepted by an audience as she had when she performed in California and Nevada.

In June 1868, while performing in her famous "nude scene," the horse Adah was bound to ran too near one of flats on the stage and the flesh of Adah's leg was torn. Later a doctor found that a cancerous growth had formed as a result of the accident. Six weeks later Adah collapsed from an advanced case of tuberculosis. She died on August 18, 1868, and was buried in Paris.

Adah was only thirty-three years old when she died. Amazingly her passing went mostly unnoticed. A brief eulogy appeared in a Paris newspaper: "Ungrateful animals, mankind; Walking his rider's hearse behind, Mourner-in-chief her horse appears, But where are all her cavaliers?"

Several months after Adah passed away, a number of her most recognized poems were printed in the September 13, 1868, edition of *Lloyd's Weekly London* newspaper. The author of the article about the accomplished actress and her poetry noted that "her name will fade out in the public mind, but it will be dug up now and again by poetic bookworms who will light upon her charming verse."

Throughout her life she professed the Jewish creed, and a few months before she died she expressed a strong desire to be buried according to the customs with nothing to mark her resting place beyond a plain piece of wood with the words, "Thou knowest."

# Leslie Carter

## The Passionate Player

*My life has run in strange places. My years have been full of color. I have known the heights of success, but likewise I have known the depths of despair.*

—Leslie Carter, *Liberty magazine*, 1927

Catherine Louise Dudley Carter sat at her desk and clutched a pen in her hand. Nothing was left of her life but the raw will to do the only quasi respectable thing open to a woman in her circumstances. She had lost the wealthy position and standing in society that she had taken for granted for so long. She'd been kicked out of her palatial home. She had failed in her divorce case and in obtaining the money to maintain her lifestyle; her nine-year-old son had been ripped from her arms, and her once good name had been scandalously linked to actor Kyrle Bellew and New York Senator James F. Pierce.

The scandal didn't bother her too much—small-minded persons, including her husband, just did not understand. "There is great romance, there is great love, there is great passion—all things difficult to guide—and some men and women reserve the right to have these things, regardless of that sharp dividing line which makes it legal," she later wrote, dramatically justifying her choices.

Unfortunately, she'd fallen to the wrong side of that sharp legal and moral dividing line and now knew the cost. Her husband, wealthy industrialist Leslie Carter, had won everything in what

30

the *New York Times*, in June 1889, called the "most indecent and revolting divorce trial ever heard in the Chicago courts." Louise Carter considered herself virtually penniless, her reputation shredded to ribbons by the press, while her husband gloated over winning his countersuit charging her with adultery.

She shuddered at the memory of the witnesses against her, a veritable parade of chambermaids, housekeepers, hotel guests, and other traitors her husband had somehow coerced into telling the most awful tales about her. He had taken everything from her. She decided to take the one thing he'd given her that could most embarrass him: his name.

The plan she conceived to become an actress did not stop short of stardom. Her name—no, his name—would be blazoned in lights for all to see. She would, forevermore, be known as Mrs. Leslie Carter. That, she thought, would make her husband's impassive face show some expression. "Nothing ever happened to Leslie Carter; consequently, nothing ever happened to his face," she recalled. The day would come she vowed, when the name she hated would be on marquee lights and his humiliation would be as great as hers was now.

Dreaming of revenge would not make it happen. Images of poverty and squalor rose in her mind. Somehow she must triumph over this ugly trick of fate that her husband and a jury had played. The theater offered the only way out, with the added attraction of mortifying her ex-husband. Shrugging away the fact that her first attempt at becoming an actress had been unsuccessful, she concocted a new plan to succeed.

Dipping her pen into a small bottle of ink, she wrote to a man who had promised to help. The plea Louise Carter sent to wealthy meatpacker Nathaniel K. Fairbank resulted in an offer to assist her to become an actress, and his influence secured an appointment with New York theatrical manager E. G. Gilmore, who agreed to handle her career.

The theater community was not just astonished by the reports that the sinful society woman intended to take to the stage; it was dumbfounded. Louise Carter had nothing much to recommend her, except, possibly, the notoriety she'd gained in the press. With no particular beauty, an astonishing amount of wild red hair, strong features, an unsavory reputation, and complete ignorance of her chosen profession, it seemed hardly feasible that she could join the ranks of Sarah Bernhardt and Lillie Langtry, reigning stars of the theater in 1889.

Her family tree showed not a twig or branch from the theatrical profession. She was born June 10, 1862, in Lexington, Kentucky. Her father was a dry goods merchant, and Catherine Louise was the younger of two children. Following her father's death when she was eight years old, her mother took the children to Dayton, Ohio, where their grandfather lived. There the lively young redhead was a student at the Cooper Seminary, where she was very popular with her classmates and the wealthy young gentlemen who came to call.

At the age of eighteen, she married the millionaire industrialist Leslie Carter, who was fourteen years her senior. The marriage was arranged by her mother and a family friend, and Catherine Louise agreed to it because it was expected. "There are certain events that arrived in due course in life," she said, and marriage was inevitable for a young woman of good family.

She returned with her husband to his hometown of Chicago, where she played her role as the wife of an important man in society. The newlyweds, however, were not alone in the Chicago mansion; Leslie Carter's brother, his aunt, and his sister also lived there.

"Here was this somber house filled to the brim with prejudices, conventionalities and prohibitions," she described later. The aunt and sister were not "bachelor girls or old maids, but spinsters." The self-described "hoyden" was "continually affronting and offending without knowing how or why."

Leslie Carter

One good thing about the divorce was that she was finally free of the family ties that had become chains. Catherine Louise Carter was pleased to think that becoming an actress would be one last, rude gesture toward her husband's family. With the newspapers screaming her name and the future uncertain at best, however, everyone, including her wealthy sponsor, considered her ideas about a career extremely improbable, so she set her sights on the one man who could make it happen.

The legendary David Belasco had earned his actor's laurels in San Francisco theater productions in the 1870s and in Virginia City, Nevada, where he first began writing plays that were moderately successful. Unfortunately his initial meeting with the society woman who thought she might like to be an actress had not gone well. He wrote, "When she first came to my attention she had no training for the stage, though as a young girl she had appeared in a number of school plays. She was bent upon becoming an actress, but she expected to start at the top. She did not have the slightest notion of what is demanded for a successful career on the stage."

Belasco had asked her whether she had in mind training for comedy or for tragedy. Her reply only confirmed his doubts about her commitment to the acting profession. "I am a horsewoman and I should like to make my first entrance on horseback jumping a high fence," she arrogantly announced.

The producer, with a reputation for withering the hopes of the pretentious, explained what it would take to prepare for a serious career in theater and was convinced at the close of their interview that he would never see Mrs. Carter behind the footlights. Thinking the matter ended, Belasco left town. He seriously underestimated her will. Showing the determination that anchored her wildly passionate nature, she set off for Belasco's rural hideaway where he was working on a play for the Lyceum Theater Company. There, on bended knee, she begged for his help. "If being hurt by people can make me act, I can act," she cried, tears rolling down her cheeks.

Belasco later described the meeting in his book *The Theater Through Its Stage Door*. Before him knelt a plain woman, he said, slender and graceful. Her hair was thick and red, her eyes green under dark eyebrows, her expression beseeching. "Nothing about her was beautiful or even pretty, but the radiance of her features, the eloquence of her soul, and the magnetism of her highly keyed, temperamental nature convinced me then and there that she would go far, if only her natural abilities were developed and controlled."

Mrs. Carter and Belasco were in some ways mirror images. He'd noted at their first meeting the intensity of her emotions, and as actor, producer, and playwright, Belasco often displayed his own remarkably intense nature. He told the story of visiting a San Francisco medical college, where he stood like a statue staring at the dissected heart of a woman who had committed suicide after resorting to prostitution. Sitting for several hours on a hard bench, gazing at the permanently still heart, he sank himself emotionally into the grief that had driven the woman to take her own life. Whenever he needed to call up deep emotional energies, he said he would picture that small heart lying silently on an autopsy table.

Using his own tried-and-true methods of evoking intense feelings, Belasco almost forcibly created an actress from a society debutant. In November 1890, after the divorce case had concluded in blaring headlines, with the, by then, reluctant backing of theatrical "angel" Nathaniel K. Fairbank, Mrs. Leslie Carter made her debut in the aptly named play *The Ugly Duckling*. The play had little to commend it in the first place and had been doctored by a professional rewrite artist; that effort not hatching a swan, Belasco added his own hand to the script.

Theater reporters agreed the play was deadly. The critics were not altogether harsh with the fledgling actress following the opening night performance. The *New York Times*, which had charged the Chicago press with yellow journalism in editorials warning that women and children should not read the newspaper accounts of the divorce, noted the scandal but acknowledged that Mrs. Carter could, in time, become a "useful actress."

Not exactly the praise that Mrs. Leslie Carter expected, but better than a barrage of overripe vegetables. Behind the scenes, however, Catherine Louise was hanging on by a thread. The wealthy pork magnate backing her career had tightened the purse strings. Belasco had not been paid, nor had the dance and voice coaches, the scenery painters, and sundry others associated with staging a production. Then, of course, there was the wardrobe she required. In a letter to Fairbank's lawyer, Charles L. Allen, she pleaded Belasco's case and then itemized her own needs: $3,000 for dresses, purchased, of course, in Europe and $140 for living expenses each month, plus the weekly charges for all her classes in singing, dancing, elocution, and so on. At the end of the list, she nobly remarked that she had gone hungry more than once but didn't mind the lack of food. All her energy was concentrated on one goal: succeeding onstage.

Enough money was scraped up to present *The Ugly Duckling*. Fairbank had cut off greater funding, and when the company took the production on the road and played to empty houses, they ended up begging their "theatrical angel" for enough money to play Chicago. He at first refused, then gave in after Belasco reportedly threatened to tell the story to the newspapers. Fairbank came up with the money. The show went on for two weeks, and Mrs. Carter netted some cash, whereas Fairbank received nothing on his investment.

Having been launched to tepid praise and after barely surviving the financially ruinous road trips at small theaters in the East, Belasco and Mrs. Carter were far from the big time. It wasn't until several years later, when she appeared in *The Heart of Maryland*, a Civil War drama written for her by Belasco, that she gained credit as a dramatic or "emotional" actress.

The play demanded a lot from a performer playing the lead in the drama Belasco had concocted, but for Mrs. Leslie Carter, drama was a way of life. In the most thrilling moment of the play, she climbed a forty-foot bell tower and grasped the bell clapper to keep it from ringing and betraying the location of the hero, who made his escape while she swung to and fro above the scenery. That scene had the audience on its feet. The play was a smash.

Unfortunately her notoriety sometimes eclipsed her performance. When the production was staged in California, the *Argonaut* recognized the actress's past even as it spoke well of her future. "The star is Mrs. Leslie Carter, who has impersonated the title role since the beginning. She began her stage career with little other capital than a divorce scandal, but she is now acknowledged to be an excellent emotional actress. How she became so we all know from Mr. Belasco's testimony in the trial he brought against Mr. Fairbank, the Chicago 'angel' who launched her in her career."

There was the bitter and the sweet in her new success. Finally the vow that she'd sworn to get even with her ex-husband was realized: "Electric lights over the theater lobbies will carry the name of Leslie Carter in five foot letters. I hate the name; consequently, I will bear it to the end. Newspapers shall spread it forth, the streets shall hum with it. Mrs. Leslie Carter! It shall be borne upon him by the printed word and the spoken word. He cannot escape. It shall hound him until his last day!"

Mr. Leslie Carter reportedly could not have cared less. "I'll never speak or listen to the mention of her name again," he announced. In later years, however, when she returned to play in Chicago, posters bearing the actress' name were kept from his sight, and he often left town during a run of her show.

At last she had her revenge. She'd lost the divorce, lost her child, lost everything but that indomitable will to get to the top. No matter what he said, she knew exactly how galling it would be to Leslie Carter to have his name a public commodity associated not with his wealth and prestige, but with his despised ex-wife's notorious lifestyle.

Perhaps her husband had misjudged her will to succeed. Without it she could not have survived Belasco's methods, as noted in the *Argonaut*'s review of *The Heart of Maryland*. Belasco had described his training of Louise Dudley Carter in a court proceeding against Fairbank, the meatpacker who had bankrolled her training as well as her first play. Although that trial took place in New York, it made headlines all over the country. Belasco, testifying in the case, said he had taken a society woman, a crude amateur, and taught her everything, from how to walk into a room to how to cry, how to read a letter, how to sit down, how to open a book—virtually every physical and emotional action, including how to breathe.

Indeed his methods were reported with great relish by the newspapers as the trial continued. His description of training Mrs. Carter to play a scene from *Oliver Twist* had the jurors gaping, according to the press. "I dragged her around by her hair, just as Bill Sykes dragged Nancy. I would hit her head on the floor and haul her about until she had reached the proper pitch and could express just what she felt."

In Belasco's view he had more than earned the money he demanded from Fairbank. "I instructed her in thirty or forty roles. She was taught fencing, boxing, wrestling, and dancing; she learned ballet and jig dancing, I taught her to be the embodiment of the poetry of motion—a great nerve trial."

At the end of the three-week court trial, Belasco was awarded only a small portion of the sum for which he sued Fairbank. The *New York Times* published a scathing editorial against the jurors and the verdict, giving Belasco sixteen thousand dollars instead of the fifty-five thousand dollars he had claimed as the trainer of a great "emotional actress."

The training may have actually been worth every penny that Belasco claimed. A few years later while Mrs. Carter was touring in the western states, the *San Francisco Chronicle* noted, "Mrs. Carter reaches a degree of febrile intensity which is tremendously effective."

After an extensive tour in 1906, Louise Carter decided to take some time off. Her red-haired son had left his father's straight-laced household as soon as he was old enough and joined his mother, despite being disinherited for deserting to the enemy camp. With her son and some friends, she traveled to the Atlantic Coast and there took a step that would dramatically change her life. While she was vacationing in Portsmouth, Massachusetts, she suddenly married actor William Louis Payne. When the news reached David Belasco, he refused to believe it. "I would as soon think of the devil asking for holy water as Mrs. Carter taking a husband," Belasco was quoted as saying when the rumors about his star began circulating.

When the gossip proved true, in perfect accord with his own dramatic reputation, Belasco telephoned the new Mrs. William Payne and told her that would be the last time she would be privileged to hear his voice. As fiercely determined as Mrs. Carter had been, he immediately began grooming a new star.

Over the next few years, without Belasco writing and producing new plays especially for her and without him drawing out every last breath of emotion possible from the actress he'd created from a willful debutante, Mrs. Carter's career declined. She performed roles Belasco had created for her in plays such as *Zaza* and *DuBarry*, but the critics were left unsatisfied.

"*DuBarry*, in which Mrs. Leslie Carter is performing at the Grand Opera House in San Francisco, is not a pleasant play; but if nothing in its plot can please—in the highest sense of the word—Mrs. Carter certainly does succeed in attracting and fascinating her auditor, and this she does by her virile force as an actress. Lacking the charm which makes Maude Adams, for instance, loved by the public, she nevertheless compels a species of admiration," wrote a reviewer in *Sunset* magazine.

The critic could not quite pinpoint what it was about Mrs. Carter that didn't quite make the grade: "Great she is not—something is lacking to that high distinction—but she so nearly attains greatness that the average witness of her acting is not quite certain whether or not she falls short of it. Only an uncomfortable conviction that something was lacking remains with him, and, even at the height of his admiration for her art, will not be dissipated."

Having started her own production company and taken her show on the road, the actress soon learned the realities of a budget. By 1908 Mrs. Carter was forced into bankruptcy, with debts amounting to nearly two hundred thousand dollars. An auction of her belongings attracted a throng of women who both admired and scorned her. The ugly divorce scandal had never completely faded away, and even her success was somehow held against her. In 1916 she announced her retirement and settled in England with her second husband, but she eventually made a comeback.

Her last really successful appearance on stage occurred in 1921. Ironically she was often competing against herself. A movie had been made of *The Heart of Maryland*, the vehicle that had made her a star, but she had no part in it. Too often her audiences were small because the movie was playing during the run of her live shows.

Bowing to the inevitable lure of the movies, she was performing character roles in Hollywood by 1931. Her son Dudley died a few years later, leaving her once more a victim of emotional anguish. One other terrible sorrow plagued her last years. She and Belasco never healed the rift caused by her marriage to William Payne. She had written her mentor repeatedly, begging for reconciliation. He refused, and once, the story goes, finding himself face-to-face in the same elevator with the actress he'd molded, he stared stonily ahead and refused to acknowledge her presence.

Gone was the admiration that had impelled Belasco to undertake the training of a society sophisticate. Erased was the memory of the "pale, slender girl with a mass of red hair and green eyes gleaming under black brows, her gestures full of unconscious grace and her voice vibrated with a musical sweetness." Gone was the convoluted dependency that had brought them both such success.

David Belasco died in May 1931 without responding to the many letters sent to him by his protégé.

She wrote a final testimonial. "We fought together years and years obstacles that seemed insurmountable, but his belief in me and my absolute sublime faith in him always helped us smile and look ahead with courage. And it seems so awful that he should have to lose this last fight." Then she quoted lines Belasco had written: "The soul is a very lonely thing—lonely comes it here—lonely goes it there—a cry at night among the trees—a glimmer in the mist that soon goes out—a little shriek of passing wind—and then it goes up on its journey—where?"

Catherine Louise Carter died in November 1937 of a heart ailment aggravated by pneumonia. Her former leading man and second husband, William Payne, the man who had come between her and Belasco, was by her side.

In 1942 Miriam Hopkins and Claude Rains starred in the movie production of *The Woman with Red Hair*, the story of the tempestuous relationship of Mrs. Leslie Carter and David Belasco.

# Catherine Hayes
## The Irish Prima Donna

*Catherine Hayes is here, delighting the people with her vocal powers, which if not of the highest order, are extremely attractive; besides which, she appears with the most unquestionable reputation—a character that is supported by her conduct and deportment here.*

—Henry Huntley, mining scout, San Francisco, 1852

A demure ten-year-old girl sat in front of a clear blue river, half ridden under a canopy of willow trees in a lush garden, singing. Her silvery-toned voice resonated across the water and filled the afternoon sky with a melancholy sound. Couples canoeing on the river paddled toward the song, halted their boats, and waited in the shadows of the trees, listening. No one said a word. Not even a whisper gave away their position to the unknowing girl. Indeed she didn't realize anyone was paying attention until she finished her tune and rapturous applause commenced. Thus was the romantic beginning of Kate Hayes's singing career.

When Catherine Hayes was born in July 1823 in Ireland, her mother, Mary, compared the child's features to those of a cherub. Her talent for singing like an angel was soon revealed.

Kate's father, Arthur, abandoned her and her sister when they were small children, leaving the family destitute; consequently, Kate and her sister were forced to go to work as soon as they were old enough. From the age of eight, Kate worked a variety of jobs, from caring for infants to scrubbing inn floors. At nineteen she found employment as an assistant to a charwoman. She sang as she cleaned the homes she worked in, and passersby who overheard her were astonished at her remarkable voice.

Bishop Edmond Knox of Limerick heard Kate singing as he was passing by one of the homes she was cleaning, and he proclaimed that she had the most beautiful voice he had ever heard. He was the first to recognize her potential and consequently took her on as his protégé. Bishop Knox consulted with friends and, along with his wife Agnus, helped raise the necessary funds to send Kate to Dublin with letters of introduction to the accomplished vocalist and voice teacher Professor Antonio Sapio.

Professor Sapio agreed to train the young girl, as her voice possessed a clearness and mellowness he had rarely heard before. One month after her arrival in Dublin, Kate made her first formal public appearance at a concert hosted by her instructor. The discriminating audience was impressed by her talent, and the reviews in the newspaper the following day reflected the crowd's pleasure. Intuitively, Sapio knew his protégé required more specialized training than he could provide and encouraged Catherine to continue her studies in France.

Bearing a letter of introduction from celebrated pianist George Osborne, Kate arrived in Paris in October 1844. Manuel Garcia, a renowned voice instructor who also taught other singers such as Jenny Lind, Maria Malibran, and Henriette Sontag, became her vocal teacher.

Garcia taught Kate everything he could, then sent her to Italy to study for a career in opera. She concentrated on language arts and drama. In Milan, she met many influential theater patrons who arranged for her to audition for Giuseppe Provini, manager of the Italian Opera in Marseilles, France. Provini was so taken by her talent that he scheduled her operatic debut on May 10, 1845, as Elvira in Bellini's opera *I Puritani*.

At the end of Kate's first performance, the audience members leapt to their feet, and bouquets of flowers filled the stage. Kate followed her debut with another stunning performance, this time in Rossini's *Moses in Egypt*.

From France she traveled to Venice, where she appeared in *Lucia di Lammermoor*. Opera lovers were enraptured by the songbird. A theater critic with the *Venetian Journal* pronounced her the "greatest living prima Donna."

In 1845 she appeared at La Scala in Milan where she sang the title role in Donizetti's *Linda di Chamounix*. Her performances in France, Venice, and Milan established her supremacy as an interpreter of Italian opera.

Now one of the most sought-after vocalists of Italian opera, "La Hayes," as her Italian fans referred to her, brought her talents to the United States early in 1851. She performed first in New York and then made the trek west to California. Theatergoers in San Francisco, anxious to see her, flooded into the American Theater Opera House. The lobby was magnificently decorated in gold and purple fabric for her performances. In 1852 *Far West News* reviewed her debut in *Le Prophete* in California:

> *Her debut has been looked forward to with considerable anxiety, both on the part of those who accompanied the fair artist to these distant shores from the theaters of her achievements in the east, and by our citizens, to whom she is introduced crowned with honors, which even "the Lind" [opera singer Jenny Lind] might envy. . . .*
>
> *To say that the American Theatre was filled would only be to confirm the expectation of every one [sic] who has heard of Catherine Hayes. The house had been re-arranged and put in excellent order for the reception of so large a company. . . . Several minutes before the opening of the concert, all the vacant places in the dress circle and parquette were filled, and one of the most intelligent and respectable audiences ever assembled within the walls of a theater in this city awaited the appearance of the star of the evening.*

Catherine Hayes

*Long and loud were the cheers and applause, which greeted her entrée. She acknowledged again and again the enthusiastic testimonial, and again and again the audience cheered and applauded. Silence having been restored, Miss Hayes sang the sweet plaintive invocation, the "Ah mon fils," (translated means "Ah, my son,") one of the most touching gems of Meyerbeer's music. It was while standing at the foot-lights, amid the storm of applause, that our citizens had the first view of Miss Catherine Hayes. . . . Miss Hayes is about thirty years of age. She is a graceful, queen-like person, of medium stature, with a fair oval face. Her features are regular, hair bright auburn, eyes blue, and her face wears an intellectual expression without much animation. She dresses with taste, and her manner is perfectly easy and self-possessed; her gesticulation appropriate and graceful.*

Catherine Hayes gave forty-two performances at the American Theatre, playing each time to a standing-room-only crowd. Tickets for the best seats in the house were auctioned for $1,125. She was one of the greatest sensations to hit the frontier.

At the close of each of her shows, hundreds of bouquets were thrown from audience members onto the stage. Occasionally those bouquets contained gold pieces, but not everyone could afford such expensive displays of admiration. So enchanted was one miner by the singer's voice (a man who no doubt spent all he had to see her perform) that he tossed his ragged hat onto the stage and cried out, "By the powers! Darling, here's my hat fer yer, and it's all I have got to give ye!"

In February 1853 Kate traveled to Sacramento to give a concert at the local Presbyterian Church. Seats for this performance were sold at auction as well, and Captain John Sutter secured a ticket for twelve hundred dollars. Author Constance Rourke attended Kate's February 8 performance and made note of how proudly Captain Sutter carried himself into the theater. He was thrilled to own the ticket for the best seat in the house. "The stout, affable old man made a conspicuous entry with a detachment of officers to the sound of thunderous applause," wrote Rourke, "and was seated with ceremony in the front row on an opulent and spacious green plush sofa."

Kate began that particular program by serenading the enthusiastic crowd with Irish ballads she'd composed herself. Later, William Michael O'Rourke, a violinist, and Monsieur Chenal, master of the clarinet, performed. Kate concluded the evening with a tearful rendition of "Home Sweet Home."

Kate ended her tour of California's Gold Country on April 18, 1853. One of her farewell recitals was held in the Alta in Grass Valley. Hundreds of people were in attendance. A glowing review of her performance appeared in the *Nevada Journal*: "The voice of the cantatrice broke forth in notes of most bewitching sweetness and harmony. The excitement of the audience increased to a furious extent, no doubt with proud ratification that they had heard for once in their lives, the voice that had awakened the admiration of the western world."

Kate delighted the citizens of Grass Valley and nearby Nevada City with her genteel demeanor and elegant style. She visited many sites in the mining towns, including a few working gold mines, and even tried panning for nuggets in one of the streams. So admired was Kate Hayes by the residents of Grass Valley that they named a street after her.

After leaving Grass Valley, Kate gave one last performance in San Francisco before boarding a steamer that would take her to Chile. A review of the San Francisco show appeared in the *Daily Alta California* on April 30, 1853: "We've seldom seen in San Francisco a finer audience than were assembled in San Francisco Hall last evening to hear Miss Hayes' last concert. The house was very full, and the walls were decorated by a line of unfortunate gentlemen who could not obtain seats. Miss Hayes was in excellent voice, no doubt inspired by the full house, and perhaps desirous of leaving a pleasant impression during her absence."

It was on her return from this great musical tour that she married William Bushell. William had been her secretary throughout, and, according to the August 17, 1861, edition of the *Times of London*, "had manifested the most disinterested zeal for her interests." However, the article continued, "The happiness of the pair was not of long duration, because William died on July 3, 1858 of 'rapid consumption.'"

From that melancholy event on, Kate spent much of her time helping those in need. Her charitable disposition, as much as her sweet voice, won for her the hearts of everyone; and it is proof of the consideration in which she was held from a social as well as from an artistic point of view.

In early 1859 Kate was struggling with health issues, and some were saying that her voice was going. But after a bit of rest she improved physically. Her returning health brought back all of the old freshness and clearness and never in her life did she pour forth her notes with richer fullness or a more profound depth of heart.

On August 11, 1861, Catherine Hayes died from a stroke. "This melancholy event will be felt by the musical world as the loss of one of its brightest ornaments, and will be deeply lamented by many who have known her amiable qualities and private worth," an article in the August 17, 1861, edition of the *Illustrated London News* read. It continued,

> Her character as an artist is well known. Highly gifted by nature, and highly accomplished by education, she excelled in every branch of her art; while in one, too, of the most delightful she was unrivalled. As a singer of national songs and ballads, those especially of her native Ireland she stood alone among all of the vocalists of the day. In music of this class, her pure beautiful voice, not strained by the efforts of the modern Italian style, was lovely; its tones were truly "wood notes wild," and her simplicity and feeling had a charm which no one could resist. In her own country, as is well known, her very name was worshipped. Wherever she went she excited an enthusiasm

*such as no singer ever created before, and the reason was that no singer ever created before, and the reason was that no singer ever was so intensely Irish.*

*Katherine Hayes, indeed, was an Irishwoman in everything—in her impulsive warmth of heart, kindliness, and generosity, as well as in her strong sense of the beautiful in music and song. Her brilliant career has been long, because it began at an early age; and she now has been cut off in the full strength and vigor of her powers, while she had still the prospect of many years of successful exertion before her. So uncertain and fleeting is human life!*

Katherine Hayes's estate was estimated at more than eighty thousand dollars.

Her contribution to the art of opera is invaluable, and she played a significant role in the development of the music and culture of frontier California. One theater critic likened her talent to a "prize of abundant worth." The *Honolulu Argus* wrote that she "could charm a soul from purgatory. In a word, she is a living Aeolian harp, tuned by the Almighty and not to be beat."

Katherine was laid to rest at the Kensal Green Cemetery in London. She was forty-two years old when she passed away.

# Sarah Kirby Stark

## The Pioneer Manager

*Ye that would have obedient wives, Beware of meddling woman's kind, officious counsel.*

—John Hambleton to the *Evening Picayune*, San Francisco, January 1851

Sarah Kirby threw down the newspaper and paced across the room, only to turn and race back to the crumpled pages. She picked them up, smoothed them out, and once again read the diatribe against her penned by John Hambleton. Sarah was stricken with grief at the suicide of Hambleton's wife. That the actor should blame *her* for his wife's untimely death and publish his accusations in the San Francisco newspapers increased her distress. Her fingers whitened, and the edges of the page crumpled as she saw herself likened to a snake squeezing the life from its victim. Hambleton wrote of his dead wife's devotion:

> *For six years of struggling hardship through poverty and sickness she was at my side night and day, with the same watchful attention as a mother to an infant, until, with the last two months a change had taken place, like a black cloud over shadowing the bright sun. She gradually lost all affection for me, riveting her attention on a female friend who, like a fascinating serpent, attracted her prey until within her coils. In silence I observed this at first, and deemed it trifling, until I saw the plot thicken.*

Sarah crushed the flimsy copy of the *Evening Picayune* again. She must counter this ugly story or lose her reputation in the city.

50

Not for this had she struggled to attain a pinnacle of success as both an actress and a theater manager. As a manager of a company of actors—one of very few women managers—bad publicity could cost her everything.

A genuine pioneer of theater in California, Sarah Kirby had made her debut in Boston but arrived in the brawling new territory within a year of the first rush of Argonauts heading for the sparkling, gold-laced streams of the Sierra. Rowe's Amphitheater in San Francisco saw her first performance as Pauline in *The Lady of Lyons.* Two months later she appeared at the Tehama Theater, which she had opened and comanaged in Sacramento. By August 1850, she was a full-fledged manager, producing plays at a theater in Stockton, and in September she was back at the Tehama in Sacramento.

Sarah was the widow of J. Hudson Kirby, also an actor. Her debut on February 21, 1850, was under her stage name, Mrs. J. Hudson Kirby. Although she performed under the name Mrs. Kirby, she was at that time married to Jacob Wingard, who died shortly thereafter in San Francisco following a fall from a horse.

The events of January 1851 threatened everything she had built in the past year. Sarah recognized the precarious position she was in after the suicide of Mrs. Hambleton and the ravings of John Hambleton in the newspapers. The Hambletons had been popular on the stage from the time of their arrival from Australia, and John Hambleton was considered one of the best comedians in the city. If readers believed Hambleton's newspaper articles, public sentiment could likely turn against Sarah, so she decided to set the record straight. Her account of the tragedy was published in the San Francisco *Daily Alta California* on January 16, 1851, the day after Hambleton's letter appeared in the *Picayune* and two days after the death of her friend:

> *Mrs. Hambleton made me her confidante, and in her*
> *statements to me at that time she represented that her*

51

*husband treated her unkindly, harshly, and by acts and language abused her to a cruel extent. About one month ago she stated to me that she had been cruelly beaten by her husband, and showed me the marks of violence upon her neck, where the marks of her husband's fingers were made when he nearly choked her to death; the skin was removed by the nails of his fingers as she extricated herself from his grasp; her head was much bruised, as she stated, from him knocking her down; and if Mrs. Smith, the landlady, had not taken him off he would have killed her.*

Theater people often lived as dramatically as the plays they appeared in, and, while some notoriety might help fill the house, Sarah knew too much infamy could turn the public away from even the best plays presented by the finest performers. Despite the harrowing tale she'd been told and the physical evidence of abuse, Sarah's newspaper account of the events said Sarah had advised Mrs. Hambleton to return to her husband.

Other newspapers contributed another angle to the tale. Having appeared frequently onstage with the very popular Hambletons, Henry Coad had apparently formed a close friendship with the battered Mrs. Hambleton. The *Daily Alta California* first mentioned Coad in the story that explained why the Jenny Lind Theater had been dark on the evening of January 14. The newspaper announced that the "favorite actress," Mrs. Hambleton, had committed suicide by drinking poison at her residence. Details were supplied in the story that followed:

*It appears that the alliance between Mr. and Mrs. Hambleton was not of a happy character, and that the latter had conceived an ardent attachment to a member of the company, Mr. Coad, who returned it with equal ardor. They had, however, determined from prudential reasons to refrain from meeting each other or conversing until some opportunity should occur when they could unite their destinies.*

Sarah Kirby Stark
COURTESY OF CAXTON PRESS

The uneasy situation had continued for some days, the newspaper reported, until Mr. Hambleton jealously accused his wife of betraying her vows. If she would tell him who it was, Hambleton reportedly had assured his wife that he would consent to a separation so that she and her lover could go their own way. Apparently believing this, she told him it was Coad, who was called to their rooms at The Bell, a rooming house where all three lived. There, Hambleton threatened to blow out his rival's brains or kill them both unless Coad departed immediately. The young man did so.

Sarah knew the agonies that the third party in this triangle was suffering. If she had advised her friend to flee with the young actor who had befriended her, would that have prevented the tragedy or only led the jealous husband to commit greater harm? The newspaper account related,

> Mrs. H., probably under the impression that [Coad] had deserted her, and been trifling with her affections merely, immediately swallowed a very large dose of some powerful corrosive poison. Medical aid was sent for as soon as it was discovered, but in about ten minutes she died. As soon as the fact that the object of his affections had poisoned herself was made known to Coad, he purchased a quantity of what he supposed was the same kind of compound, and attempted to poison himself. An emetic was administered soon after, and at last accounts he was doing well, although suffering severely.

The funeral cortege had barely passed the doors of the Parker House and the darkened Jenny Lind Theater before a new bombshell hit the papers. John Hambleton's accusation against Sarah Kirby was printed in the *Evening Picayune*, complete with details of his wife's terrible death, his actions, and a final finger pointing at the woman he blamed for the whole thing: "I therefore, from my heart, attribute the cause of insanity to the evil counsels of Mrs. Kirby, and forgive the young man Coad, whose every action I have most acutely, though silently watched; for he was a victim as well as my poor wife."

Sarah could not let that indictment stand. Many people would not read between the lines and understand that Hambleton's obsessive watching of his wife's every move was as diabolically inclined as it had been, nor would they understand that his poor wife had suffered the violence that Hambleton had not meted out to Coad. If Sarah Kirby were to retain her standing, and her lease on the Jenny Lind, she would have to convince the world that she was not to blame.

Sarah recognized that even in rambunctious California a serious actress and theater manager absolutely had to exhibit an exceptional character or risk alienating theater patrons. Rip-roaring Frisco was taking steps toward a more civilized image. The editor of the *Golden Era* magazine offered a blunt warning about the danger of corruption from the stage. He uncompromisingly suggested that "all persons of the theatrical profession" should have to provide a certificate of good character before being allowed to perform before the public.

In the short amount of time she'd spent in the area, Sarah had acquired a reputation for hard work and for providing the best theater fare in the city. This was reflected in an opinion in the *Daily Alta California*: "Since she has been with us in this city, she has spared neither time, labor nor expense in presenting for the public a series of dramatical entertainments characterized by discriminating taste and sterling ability. Sarah's skill as an actress was the cornerstone for the theater company she created. As manager, Sarah made all the decisions. She hired and paid for the theater, designed sets, chose costumes, and selected actors. The problems of her actors became her own. Her "good character" at a time when women in the theater were often considered one step up from prostitutes was essential to her success—as well as the paychecks and reputations of those in her troupe."

California took its theater seriously, according to witnesses like Frank Marryat, an Englishman who traveled extensively and wrote of his adventures. "Perhaps in no other community so limited could one find so many well-informed and clever men—men of all nations, who have added the advantages of traveling to natural abilities and a liberal education," Marryat wrote of the gold miners arriving by the thousands from all over the world. There was a level of sophistication and unexpectedly puritan point of view when it came to serious drama that threatened Sarah and her company of actors.

Late in the week of the tragedy, other witnesses told their stories to the press, corroborating Sarah's version of the events that had ended in death for her friend and near death for another fine actor in her company.

The true test of public reaction to the scandal occurred a few days later, when Sarah appeared at the Jenny Lind. Tension among the troupe was high. No one could predict what would happen when the curtain rose. The *Daily Alta California* reported that friends of Mr. Hambleton were expected to create such a disturbance that Sarah Kirby would be unable to perform: "The theater was filled soon after the doors were open, and upon the appearance of Mrs. Kirby in the character of Florinda in *The Apostate*, she was received in the most generous and hearty manner."

An attempt by half a dozen people to hiss and boo the actress was quelled soon after it began. Following the final act, the same newspaper reported that the audience rewarded her with applause long and deep and unanimous. "She made a few appropriate remarks, which coming from her heart, found a channel to the hearts of the audience, and when she retired [for the evening] she received a regular storm of cheers. This was right, and we have now a higher respect for the American heart than we had before, if that is possible."

The newspaper also pointed out that the scandal had threatened the viability of the troupe. The loss of three performers meant that two other women in the company had to play men's parts. The performance, however, passed the test of San Francisco's theater critics and the public.

Having confirmed her respectability, Sarah continued to produce plays and present her customary roles. She appeared in a number of Shakespeare's most popular plays and acted in the light comedy that often completed an evening's entertainment.

Back in Sacramento that spring, Sarah opened the Tehama Theater for a benefit for local fire companies, all manned by unpaid volunteers. The *Sacramento Daily Union* praised theater managers James Stark and Sarah Kirby: "We have never known the managers of a theater exhibit a greater disposition to contribute to the advancement of charitable objects, or those measures which in our city cannot be sustained except by private donation."

She and the leading man in her troupe were married in June 1851 in Sacramento. Sarah and James Stark, a handsome man with an established reputation as an actor, completed their theatrical engagement on the evening of their wedding, then took a "matrimonial tour" to Marysville, a major center for miners headed for the gold-laced foothills some thirty miles away. James was described by fellow actor Walter Leman as "an admirable actor . . . a man of kind and generous feelings."

Sarah's newest husband, her third, had come to San Francisco late in 1850 and immediately established a reputation as a fine Shakespearean actor. James was especially successful with his role in *King Lear*, which was frequently lauded in newspapers. As a couple, Sarah Kirby Stark and James Stark were also recognized as "the first to render the theater in California an institution worthy of the support of an intellectual and refined public."

As an accomplished performer, Sarah played tragedy and comedy with equal expertise. She was praised in the *Daily Alta California* for her contributions to theater in her first years in California. "She is our pioneer actress, and for the three years during which California has sprung almost from a wilderness to a proud State, she has labored incessantly to raise the drama to its present position among us."

Still she was careful of her reputation. In 1852, more than a year after the Hambleton affair that had so tested her courage, she played a man's role in *The Iron Chest*. A woman in trousers almost guaranteed a full house, yet Sarah was not comfortable, and some laughter from the front rows threw her off stride. At the conclusion of the play, her husband appeared and apologized for an uneven performance, caused, he said, "by the novelty of her dress." According to the *San Francisco Herald*: "The audience immediately responded with hearty denials and chanted for the appearance of Sarah, who, when the tumult subsided, explained that necessity alone had induced her to take the part and wear the infamous trousers, there being no male actor available."

Over the next decade and more, Sarah continued to perform in theaters throughout California and in other western states. Sometimes she and her husband appeared together; sometimes they played roles in separate venues in disparate locations.

In Shakespeare's last, great tragedy, *Richard III*, both James and Sarah were recognized for their skills after a performance in Nevada City in 1857. According to a critic in the *Nevada Journal*, "Mrs. Stark, it is superfluous to say, rendered most thrillingly the character of the Duchess of York—one so difficult that Shakespeare has often doubted if such a character could have existed in life."

Sarah returned to San Francisco several times, always bringing plays the public and critics applauded. Her company was praised by newspapers for the quality of the players, the dramas and comedies that were staged, and for the respectable lifestyle of its manager. Part of that was attributable to the benefits that she held to raise money for things like a hospital and churches. James, however, found the lure of the gold mines irresistible. He made a comfortable income as a miner, and when he died he left behind a quartz mill bearing his name in the remote canyon between Aurora and Bodie, California.

Once again Sarah was a widow, but James Stark's success at gold mining left her comfortably well off. All was not well, however. According to a lawsuit, Sarah was soon victimized in a property transaction. The property Sarah reportedly conveyed to her niece and husband carried a condition that they care for the aging actress as a member of the family. The *San Francisco Call* published a story in 1883 that detailed an action Sarah filed to recover the title to the home on the corner of Twenty-Fourth Street and San Jose Avenue. The report says that for many years Sarah had been an invalid, dependent upon the seventy-five-dollar monthly rent from the house. She had, reported the newspaper, "on two different occasions dislocated her hip, which has rendered her weak in body and mind, dependent and lonely and greatly in need of a home, kind care, and attention and society such as only relatives can bestow." The relatives in question apparently consigned her to a back room, and, when she felt compelled to leave, she was told never to return, even to remove her belongings.

She may have been "lonely" in May when the property changed hands, but by September she was married again, to another actor, Charles Thorne, whom she had initially met years before. According to old newspapers, the two veterans toured Australia and the Orient and "did a good business."

Sarah died in December 1898. She had returned to San Francisco after Thorne's death, and the *San Francisco Chronicle* published a short piece noting that she was "a woman well known here in the early days as an actress of considerable ability."

# Charlotte Cushman

## The Actress in Trousers

*Perhaps it was the reverses against which Charlotte Cushman*
*so successfully struggled and the will power and determination*
*which were hers during her difficulties that gave her the person-*
*ality and ability to be America's greatest actress.*

—*BRADFORD ERA NEWSPAPER,*
FEBRUARY 22, 1923

It was a cold evening in the early spring of 1859 when the well-known actress Charlotte Cushman debuted in Shakespeare's *Hamlet* at the Metropolitan Theatre in San Francisco. The city's most wealthy and influential people arrived by carriage. Throngs of curious bystanders eager to see the aristocrat hovered around the walkway leading into the building. The fine, brick edifice rivaled the most notable on the East Coast.

Inside, the grand hall was fitted with the most ornate fixtures and could seat comfortably upward to a thousand people. From the private boxes to the gallery, every part of the immense building was crowded to excess. Charlotte Cushman was recognized by theatergoers as the "greatest living tragic actress," and everyone who was anyone wanted to see her perform. Several women had won fame with their impersonations of male characters in various dramas, but critics and fans alike regarded Charlotte as the best of them all.

In 1845 a theatrical reviewer in London had written about one of Charlotte's performances in glowing terms. "Miss

Cushman's Hamlet must henceforth be ranked among her best performances. Every scene was warm and animated, and at once conveyed the impression of the character. There was no forced or elaborate attempt at feeling or expression. You were addressed by the whole mind; passion spoke in every feature, and the illusion was forcible and perfect."

The audience that flocked to see the exceptionally talented Charlotte in California that evening was treated not only to a "forcible and perfect" interpretation of *Hamlet*, but also to a display of the actress's temper.

Charlotte and her supporting cast played to an enraptured house for the first half of the production. Actors maneuvered themselves in and out of the elaborate set that consisted of a castle and turrets on the right side of the stage and imposing cliffs rising out of the fog on the left side. The simulated sounds of wind wailing through the crevices of stone and of the sea crashing against the rocky shore added to the drama. During a particular scene between Hamlet and Ophelia, Hamlet's intended wife, a man in the audience sneezed loudly and with a long, drawn-out *cach-oo!*

Charlotte stopped and stared at the man. Then, quietly leading the actress playing Ophelia off the stage, she approached the footlights and said in a loud tone, "Will someone put that person out?" Everybody sat still. "If some gentleman doesn't, I will," Charlotte announced rolling up her sleeves. The individual got up and sneaked out of the theater. Only after the audience had turned its full attention back to Charlotte did she proceed with the play.

From the moment Charlotte entered the field of entertainment in 1829 at the age of thirteen, she was serious about her craft. According to her biographer and for a time her significant other, Emma Stebbins, Charlotte had a remarkable voice and an uncanny ability to perfectly imitate the tones, movements, and expressions of those around her. Charlotte confessed she inherited her talent for singing from her mother. "She sang all the songs of the time with good voice and taste, and I learned to love music in the truest way at a mother's side," Charlotte shared with Emma.

Charlotte was born in Boston in 1816. Her father was in the West Indies goods trade. Her mother was an artist who enjoyed painting and poetry. Charlotte, by her own admission, was a "tomboy" who liked to climb trees and build things using her uncle's tools. "I was very destructive to toys and clothes, tyrannical to my brothers and sister, but very social and a great favorite with other children," she pontificated about her youth.

Charlotte's uncle, her mother's brother, introduced her to the theater. He owned stock in the Tremont Theatre in Boston and would often take Charlotte to plays and musicals. Just before Charlotte became a teenager, her father lost everything in a poor financial investment. The Cushmans were forced to move from Boston to an area where the children could find work to support the family. Charlotte earned a living singing. A friend of her father's helped her get the proper training she needed to find a job as a vocalist. She sang with a number of orchestras and choirs and for seven years learned the science of music. While she was practicing a solo at a piano manufacturer, a theatrical representative came in to purchase a piano. He was taken by Charlotte's talent. "Her voice was a very remarkable one," Emma Stebbins wrote of her companion. "It had almost two registers, a full contralto and almost a full soprano, but the low voice was the natural one." The theatrical representative took Charlotte as a client.

Charlotte's operatic debut occurred in 1835 at the Tremont Theatre, where she played Countess Almavia in the *Marriage of Figaro*. After a successful showing in Boston, she traveled to New Orleans to perform at the St. Charles Theatres. It was while portraying Lucy Bertram in *Guy Mannering* that an unfortunate event occurred that altered the course of her career. Charlotte recalled in her memoirs:

*Owing perhaps to my youth, change of climate, or strain of the show itself, I found my voice failing me. In my un-happiness I went to ask counsel and advice of the manager of the chief New Orleans theatre. He at once said to me, "You ought to be an actress and not a singer." He invited me to study some parts, and presented me to Mr. Barton, the tragedian of the theatre, who he asked to hear me, and to take an interest in me. After a short time, he was suf-ficiently impressed with my powers to propose that I should play Lady Macbeth at a benefit the theatre was to present.*

Not only was Charlotte's professional life taking a dra-matic turn, but personally she was dealing with changes as well. According to the February 23, 1912, edition of the *Daily Crescent News,* Charlotte was romantically involved with fellow thespian Conrad Clark. They had met while performing in the same troupe in Boston, and Charlotte believed they had a promising future. It wasn't until after appearing at the New Orleans Theater that she learned otherwise. One night during one of the shows, a strange woman carrying a small child caught up to Charlotte behind the scenes between the acts. "You are Charlotte Cushman, the great promising star of the stage?" the woman began curtly. "Haven't you got enough men to admire you without coming between man and wife and robbing me of my husband?"

"Your husband?" Charlotte inquired.

"Yes, and you have taken or are trying to take him from me," the woman continued.

"Who is your husband?" Charlotte asked.

"Conrad Clark," replied the woman, "the father of my child." Charlotte stared back at the woman as though she had been shot.

She excused herself and finished the remainder of the show. Once the performance had ended, she sent for Clark to come to her dressing room. Clark knocked and then opened the door. She brought forth to him his wife and baby, waiting there to see him. Clark tried to explain, but Charlotte wasn't interested in hearing

Charlotte Cushman as Meg Merrilies in the play *Guy Manning*

what he had to say. She escorted the Conrads out and proceeded to have a good cry.

Charlotte decided to put Clark out of her mind and threw herself into studying the part of Lady Macbeth with all the enthusiasm and industry that were hers. She played Lady Macbeth with such feeling that the theater manager asked her to continue the part for the remainder of the season. Charlotte was well received everywhere she performed. Her work as Lady Macbeth led to a variety of other acting jobs including portraying Romeo in *Romeo and Juliet*. According to an article in the April 8, 1837, edition of the *Boston Morning Post*,

> *Miss Charlotte Cushman was captivating.*
>
> *At the close of the play, a very beautiful wreath was thrown on the stage, which was placed on the head of the fair beneficiary by the manager of the theatre, who led Charlotte forward to receive accolades from the audience. The deafening shouts of applause which followed this compliment were proof that only one feeling pervaded the highly respectable assemblage in attendance.*
>
> *Miss Cushman is about leaving us, but we hope only for a short time, as we are certain she has no warmer friends, nor anyone who will hail her return with more real pleasure.*

Charlotte's successful performances were noticeable incidents. She traveled to Philadelphia, New York, and Detroit, starring in a variety of engagements in which her versatility as a performer was recognized by all. In the winter of 1842, she undertook the management of the Walnut Street Theatre in Philadelphia. She proved to have a talent for selecting quality plays and performers to act the parts. Charlotte took on many of the roles herself, adding to her repertoire and increasing her knowledge of acting. After nearly two years serving as a theater manager, she decided to focus all her energy in studying performing. Shakespearean actor and theater manager William Charles Macready hired Charlotte to be a part of his acting troupe. She learned every aspect of the profession from walk-on roles to starring vehicles. The education proved invaluable.

In a letter to a friend during this period of her life, Charlotte shared what would become sound advice for many actresses to come. She wrote, "I have become aware that no one could ever sail a ship by entering at the cabin windows: he must serve and learn his trade before the mast. This is the way I would henceforth learn mine."

In late 1844 William signed his troupe to a tour of Europe. In 1845 Charlotte debuted in London as Bianca in *Fazio* at the Princess Theatre. The reviews she received from the *London Times* were glowing. "The great characteristics of Miss Cushman are her earnestness, her intensity, her quick apprehension of readings, her power to dart from emotion to emotion with the greatest rapidity, as if carried on by impulse alone," the May 18, 1845, edition of the newspaper reported. "We need hardly say that Miss Cushman is likely to prove a great acquisition to the London stage. For passion, real, impetuous, irresistible passion, she has not at present her superior. At the end of the play Miss Cushman, who had acted throughout with great applause came forward and was received with showers of bouquets; never were bouquets more richly merited."

While touring Europe, Charlotte took a number of male roles in classic plays. She was joined on stage by her sister Susan. The two often played Romeo and Juliet, with Susan portraying Juliet opposite Charlotte's Romeo. Susan became a full-time part of the theater world after her husband abandoned her and their child. Charlotte took her sister and nephew in and cared for them. The Cushman sisters had a reputation for providing theatergoers with moving performances. According to the British newspaper the *English Gentlemen*, audiences had an "exceptional interest" in the Miss Cushmans and while performing at the Adelphi Theatre in Liverpool "more than 1,200 people were received at the doors, the half of the sum earned from ticket sales was paid to the ladies."

During the four years Charlotte traveled Europe, she attained a degree of celebrity no other American had achieved prior to her. "She is likely to become still more distinguished among us," a notice in the October 31, 1849, edition of the *London Daily News* noted, "for it is long, very long, since an actress possessing so much talent appeared upon the English stage."

Charlotte's career abroad thrived, but she suffered a number of setbacks with her health. She was tired and experienced pain in her chest and abdomen. It would be years before doctors would discover she was struggling with cancer. Although she seldom canceled a performance due to illness, she did require time to rest between new shows. At times the look of exhaustion she wore was visible to the press. The May 16, 1846, edition of the *English Gentlemen* reported that "at the termination of the tragedy [the type of play she was performing], Miss Charlotte Cushman was attacked by indisposition, attendant on her late professional exertions."

Charlotte's private life contributed to her "indisposition" on occasion. She was involved with a number of women in what were referred to as "strong female friendships." In the summer of 1843, Charlotte became romantically involved with Rosalie Sully, the daughter of the artist she hired to paint her portrait. For more than a year, the two were inseparable. The letters Charlotte kept between the two were passionate and spoke of the long life the pair hoped to share together. According to Charlotte's diary, she gave Rosalie a ring in July 1844, and the two were subsequently married the same month. The legality of their union is a matter of question, but what is clear is the strong bond the couple enjoyed.

Life as a traveling thespian eventually took a toll on Charlotte and Rosalie's relationship. They grew apart, and Charlotte began seeing someone else. News that Charlotte had a new lover broke Rosalie's heart. She sank into a severe depression and remained in the forlorn state until her death in 1847. When Charlotte was informed of Rosalie's demise, she suffered a mental collapse. She canceled her spring tour and retreated to a spa in Switzerland. Charlotte and musical critic Henry Charley exchanged letters while she was away in which he described what she needed to do to return to the stage. "Keep yourself tranquil, hopefully in lavender, both mind and body, and get as much rest, health, and strength as you can," Henry instructed. "When you come again to London you are right in thinking that you must come well."

Charlotte did not return to the stage until the summer of 1848. According to the October 31, 1849, edition of the *London Express,* Charlotte played for crowded houses for some time and with eminent success. "We have been told she plans to return to the American stage and will certainly be enthusiastically welcomed back," the article read.

Charlotte returned to America in 1850, and theaters from Boston to San Francisco sought to have her perform in the city's finest playhouses. The November 2, 1850, edition of the *Atlas London Middlesex* announced that she was "drawing immense houses in New York." Charlotte received favorable reviews everywhere she performed. Her exceptional acting skills were reported across the states, along with stories about her personal life. Her romance with Matilda Hays was the subject of several articles. Matilda was a journalist, writer, and part-time actress. The two were frequently seen in public together dressed in matching clothing. The August 30, 1851, edition of the *Daily Alta California* noted that Charlotte had "adopted the male attire—hat, coat, and trousers, it is believed permanently and prefers the company of women in particular the company of novelist Matilda Hays."

Charlotte and Matilda became involved after meeting in London in 1849. When Charlotte left Europe for America,

Matilda accompanied her. They would occasionally raise the eyebrows of strangers who objected to their relationship. An article in the July 31, 1851, edition of the *Cleveland Plaindealer* noted that both women were frequently seen holding hands and were dressed in a "manner most offensive." The article detailed,

> *Miss Cushman and her companion astonished the guests of the Ste. Marie Hotel one fine morning by appearing cap-a-pie in masculine clothing, hat, coat, unmentionables and all. You who have seen her personation of Hamlet can easily understand the grace and ease with which she wore her "toggery." Here was not a single motive of triumph: not a mere desire to astonish: the dinner-table, and then, like a ghost of Banquo, to vanish away and go back to petticoats and whalebone. No, she rode in it, fished, walked, ran and romped in it, and for ought that we can learn, has determined to wear it for the remainder of her days, at least, of maidenhood.*

Charlotte and Matilda were together for five years.

The *Sacramento Daily Union* kept fans of the actress in the west updated on the various venues where she performed; New Orleans, Savannah, Charleston, Washington, Baltimore, and Philadelphia were all locations Charlotte played during her tour of the East Coast. The February 3, 1852, edition of the *Sacramento Daily Union* announced that Charlotte was "expected to arrive in this part of the country shortly." Charlotte's arrival in the Gold Country was delayed in order for her to recover from surgery she'd had on her foot. She'd injured her foot while running and needed an operation to remove a bone fragment. While convalescing, she decided to retire from the stage. It was an idea she had been considering for some time.

On Saturday, May 1, 1852, Charlotte gave her farewell performance in Philadelphia before departing for Europe. She told reporters and her devoted followers that "she had been eighteen years on the stage, and had made money enough to retire and give place to others." Charlotte and Matilda settled in Rome surrounded by friends who were artists and writers and who readily accepted the relationship the couple shared. They immersed themselves in a world of progressive painters and poets and read new works by authors who embraced alternative lifestyles such as sculptor Harriet Hosmer and writer Grace Greenwood. During this time Charlotte had her portrait done by American painter William Page. Page's portrait is recognized by art historians as one of his finest works. It inspired Charlotte's friend, poet and artist Benjamin Paul Ahlers, to write of the painting:

> *He who is worthy of the privilege [to see Page's work] stands suddenly conscious of the presence such as the world has rarely known. He sees too, the possibilities of the near future, how from that fine equipoise the soul might pass out into rare manifestations, appearing in the sweetness and simplicity of a little child, in the fearful tumultuousness of Lady Macbeth, in the passionate tenderness of Romeo, or in the gothic grandeur of the Scotch sorceress; in the love of kindred, in the fervor of friendship, and in the nobleness of the truest womanhood.*

After a brief affair with Grace Greenwood, Charlotte and Matilda parted company. Charlotte then began a romance with sculptor Emma Stebbins. The two met at the reading of a new talent's play, a writer who believed he was akin to Shakespeare. "She never let on how his crude efforts must have struck her cultivated sense," Emma wrote in her memoirs. "There was a winning charm about her far above mere beauty of feature, a wondrous charm of expression and sympathy which took all hearts and disarmed criticism."

Shortly after Charlotte and Emma moved in together, Charlotte traveled back to America for a short tour. From the spring of 1857 to the summer of 1858, she appeared in theatrical venues from coast to coast. Charlotte performed in the usual works of Shakespeare, which included playing the part of Cardinal Wolsey in *Henry VIII*. She was joined on stage by such well-known actors as Peter Richings and Edwin Booth. News of her successful engagements back in her native homeland was reported in the *Sacramento Daily Union* and the *Daily Alta California*.

In May 1858 an accident occurred while Charlotte was performing in *Macbeth* in Nashville, Tennessee, that could have ended her career had she not kept a clear head. According to the May 31, 1858, edition of the *Sacramento Daily Union*, it happened during the sleeping scene in the fifth act of the play. The article read,

> *As Lady Macbeth approaches from her chambers, lamp in hand, the light lace veil with which Miss Cushman's head and shoulders were covered, caught fire and blazed like tinder. Miss Cushman without relaxing a muscle of fixed features, or showing by any visible sign the least discomposure, caught the blazing robe in her grasp and immediately extinguished it, without turning her eyes either right or left, or betraying the least sign of emotion of any kind. So promptly and fearlessly was it done, and so much was it in keeping with the character she was playing, that not with-standing the distinguished audible shrieks of some of the ladies, many present actually believed it to be a part of the performance. It certainly was one of the greatest pieces of acting we ever witnessed.*

Many newspaper articles praising Charlotte's acting were written by Grace Greenwood. Her infatuation with the celebrated thespian was clear in the reports Grace wrote in advance of Charlotte's arrival in various cities. Perhaps Grace hoped the positive items she contributed about the actress would counter any negative notices others might offer. The fact that Charlotte was a lesbian was a source of gossip from time to time, and those who objected to her sexual orientation posted comments about whom she was seeing. The February 14, 1859, edition of the *Sacramento Daily Union* reported that Charlotte was involved with Harriet

Hosmer, and the *New Albany Weekly* edition claimed she was in a relationship with an eighteen-year-old actress named Emma Crow. An article in the December 6, 1859, edition of the *Sacramento Daily Union* offered an unflattering report from an actor meeting Charlotte in October 1842:

> *She was by no means then the actress which she after-wards became. She displayed at that time a rude, strong, uncultivated talent. At that time she was frequently careless in the text and negligent of rehearsals. She played the Queen to me in Hamlet and I recollected her shocking my ear and very much disturbing my impres-sion of the reality of the situation by her saying to me in the closet scene, "What will thou do? Thou will not kill me." Instead of, "What wilt thou do? Thou wilt not murder me?" Thus sustaining a weak word for a strong one, diluting the force, and destroying the rhythm of the verse. She was much annoyed at her error when I told her of it.*

By the end of 1859, Charlotte was back in Italy, where the subject of her personal life was not an issue. She and Emma Stebbins entertained friends and family at their home in Rome and spent time riding their stable of horses and gardening. Between 1860 and 1873, Charlotte traveled back and forth from Europe to America three times to perform onstage in the roles she had become famous for portraying. Between shows Charlotte would give impromptu acting lessons to the young players in the cast who aspired to be as skilled in the acting profession. According to Emma Stebbins's biography, Charlotte was generous to fellow thespians on and off the stage and had a great deal to teach.

Emma later recalled in writing:

> *Behind the scenes is such a terra incognita to the world at large, that few are able to judge righteous judgment from the standpoint of personal experience. To those who have this experience it ought to be a duty as well as a pleasure to speak a word in season for a much misunderstood and*

*ill-judged class, who have inherited the prejudices of ages, and yet have been able to show so many shining examples of genius and goodness to the admiration of the world.*

*It was one of Miss Cushman's crowning glories that she knew how to reconcile the inconsistencies and harmonize the discordances of this peculiar realm, where she reigned with the same undoubted sovereignty as everywhere else. Her mere presence on the stage seemed to give life and value to what was too often a mere collection of incongruous materials. Her earnestness, and her thoroughness seemed to be once infused into the mass of inertia, ignorance, and indifference; all had to do their best, because she always did her best; and her best was not, as in so many instances, a mere ego, stalking around, wrapped in its own sublime self-confidence, looking down upon and ignoring the lesser lights as of no consequence. Her artistic ideal was of a different sort; she knew and felt the absolute truth of the old, time-honored law that "God hath set the members every one of them in the body, as it hath pleased him. . . . That there should be no schism in the body, but that the members should have the same care one for another. . . . And whether one member suffers, all the members suffer with it; or one member be honored, all the members rejoice with it. And she could not see anything working wrongly or ignorantly, without doing her very best to right it. Her rehearsals were always hard-working lessons to all about her; and that in no unkind or harsh spirit, but with all the kindly helpfulness of her nature, suggesting, encouraging, showing how a thing ought to be done, and, when she saw the true spirit of endeavor and improvement, giving it a cheering word which was invaluable.*

In 1874 Charlotte gave the first of three farewell performances in *Macbeth* at Booth's Theatre in New York. At the end of the play, the fifty-eight-year-old distinguished actress was presented with a laurel wreath and afterward escorted to the Fifth Avenue Hotel for an elaborate dinner and serenade from a local choir.

Between times portraying Queen Katherine, Meg Merrilieses, or Lady Macbeth, Charlotte enjoyed outings with her friends. Her excursions were covered by newspapers such as the *Edwardsville Intelligencer* of Illinois. The June 30, 1875, edition noted that the "tragediennes are often tragic without meaning to be." The article continued,

> It has been related that Miss Charlotte Cushman was recently riding in a Hartford horse car, when, thinking she arrived at her destination, she turned to her neighbor and asked in her deep tone, in which there was more of Katherine of England than is usually heard on horse cars, "This is Pleasant Street, is it not?" The lady addressed, who was not only a friend but a fan of Charlotte's work, seized her dramatic opportunity with equally tragic effect, and replied, "It is." There was a roar of merriment in which Miss Cushman joined as heartily as any.

Her next engagement was at the Globe Theatre in Boston. Audiences enjoyed a two-week run of the characters she played from *Macbeth* to *Guy Mannering*. She took her final bow at the popular Massachusetts venue on May 29, 1875.

On July 7, 1875, the *Indianapolis Journal* reported that Charlotte had "taken ill" but was resting comfortably at her summer home in Newport, Massachusetts. The July 9, 1875, edition of the *Logansport Daily Pharos* reported that she was "dying." The article explained that in truth she was not suffering from a disease or physical ailment, only "sick of the business." Charlotte vehemently denied the claim and assured her public that she "enjoyed acting now as much as she ever did."

An editor at the *Newport Daily News* was pleased to learn that Charlotte's enthusiasm for the art had not been diminished. He maintained in an article from August 2, 1875, that the likes of someone with Charlotte's talent would not come around again. "Such gifts do not belong to every generation; they are the aloes of genius and blossom perhaps once in a hundred years." "We can't help looking for those true workers, the correct interpreters of art, the honest, earnest lovers of the stage," the article continued.

"Thirty-five years ago Charlotte Cushman with her plain, highly intellectual, soul-illuminated face, by reason of the fire that was in her, the fever and passion of art that absorbed her, was able to conquer circumstances and make herself the Queen of the American stage, beloved at home, and honored abroad."

By November 1875, Charlotte was in Philadelphia delivering readings from plays and giving lectures on the art of acting. She had been struggling with poor health again and for a while required assistance to walk. She recovered enough to stand on her own to take the stage in Easton, Pennsylvania. It was there that she made her last public appearance. Her efforts were appreciated by many who attended her engagements. One admirer wrote Charlotte in December 1875:

> *Let me tell you of the entire and perfect success of last evenings' reading. My most critical judgment could not pick a flaw in you or your work. You looked and did superbly. It is the praise of modern things that in your half-dozen selections you could gather up such sweet and noble sentiments, and that you could succeed, either in getting out of it or putting into it, such exquisite shadings of thought and feeling. I was never among a more impressed and delighted audience . . .*

Charlotte returned to Massachusetts and died of pneumonia at the Parker House in Boston on February 18, 1876. News of Charlotte's death was widely reported. Information about the actress began to surface. The February 21, 1876, edition of the *Janesville Gazette* reported,

> *Charlotte Cushman, the greatest of female histrionic artists of past or present times, is dead. After years of study and toil, success and crowning victories, sickness and continued pain, she passed away this morning at her hotel.*
>
> *Charlotte Cushman was never married. Her life was too busy for such a step, and she seemed possessed with one great desire to become queen of no condition but that of*

*her art. She possessed many peculiarities of character, one of which was her strict watchfulness of financial matters. In later life she always demanded the theatre manager's portion of the engagement money in the midst of each evening's performances. She would rarely play for the many benevolent enterprises brought to her notice, but during the late war her patriotism showed forth in brightest colors, her performances for the benefit of the United States Sanitary Commission netting many thousands of dollars. Her earnings have been very great, and she must have a vast fortune.*

Emma Stebbins let it be known in her memoirs that in the spring of 1869 Charlotte had been diagnosed with a malady that was later defined as breast cancer. She underwent a series of treatments that only temporarily stopped the growth of the tumor physicians in Rome and England had tried to eradicate. "The snake was only scotched, not killed," Emma wrote.

Charlotte's funeral was held on February 21, 1876. Hundreds of her friends, including the highest dignitaries of the Commonwealth, members of the profession that she loved so well, and a large number of her fellow citizens were present. According to the February 22, 1876, edition of the *Boston Post*: "The actress's body was placed in a casket covered with black cloth and ornamented with silver trimmings. In her folded hands was placed a spray of lilies of the valley and upon the casket ivy and a beautiful star formed of red and white carnations bordered with violets, and at the head of the coffin stood a large floral crown." Charlotte's body was taken to King's Chapel, where the service was held.

The *Boston Post* article noted that,

*The galleries were reserved for ladies and for a long time before the hour for beginning the ceremonies every seat in the place and the body of the church not reserved for the relatives and intimate friends of the deceased was occupied. The floral decorations were numerous and elegant in design and material, from a bed of white roses and pond lilies, upon which the words in violet "Fare Thee Well" arose a column holding a crown surmounted by a cross.*

Charlotte was buried at the Mount Auburn Cemetery in Boston. A crowd of one hundred people followed the pallbearers carrying her casket from the hearse to her final resting place. Bereaved friends passed by the spot to pay their final respects. Charlotte was lowered into the section of ground she had selected for herself several months earlier and the grave was closed.

The honored actress was always grateful for the outpouring of affection she received. She had a habit in her career of graciously thanking people for their kind response to her work. In 1874 she had offered a few words to an audience that had given her a standing ovation after a performance at Booth's Theatre. The words of thanks Charlotte expressed to her adoring public then might have been the words she would have shared with those at her funeral who loved her to the end:

*Beggar that I am, I am even poor in thanks, but I thank you. Gentlemen, the heart has no speech; its only language is a tear or a pressure of the hand, and words very feebly convey or interpret its emotions. Yet I would beg you to believe that in the three little words I now speak, "I thank you," there are heart depths which I should fail to express better, though I should use a thousand other words. I thank you, gentlemen, for the great honor you have offered me. I thank you, not only for myself, but for my whole profession, to which, through and by me, you have paid this very graceful compliment. If the few words I am about to say savor of egotism or vainglory, you will, I am sure, pardon me, inasmuch as I am here only to speak of myself. You would seem to compliment me upon an honorable life. As I look back upon that life, it seems to me that it would have been impossible for me to have led any other. In this I have, perhaps, been mercifully helped more than are many of my more beautiful sisters in art. I was, by a press circumstances, thrown at an early age into a profession for which I had received no special edu-cation or training; but I had already though so young, been brought face to face with necessity. I found life sadly real and intensely earnest, and in my ignorance of other ways of study. I resolved to take there from my text and my watchword. To be thoroughly in earnest, intently in earnest in all my thoughts and in all my actions, whether in my profession or out of it, became my one single idea. And I honestly believe herein lies the secret of my success in life. I do not believe that any great success in any art can be achieved without it.*

Charlotte Cushman was fifty-nine years old when she died.

# Sarah Bernhardt

## The Divine Sarah

*With what the inhabitants of former worlds compared the sun, I
know not; and with whom the present generation may compare
Bernhardt, I know as little.*

—THE WAVE, MAY 2, 1891

The pliant figure leaned over the ship's rail, expressive eyes
intent on the blue-green waters of the harbor. A mass of wavy
light-brown hair with tints of gold lifted and curled with every
breeze, its arrangement a matter of complete indifference to the
angler. Suddenly the slender form froze, breath held, and then,
with a quick yank and a breaking smile, lifted the rod and hauled a
wriggling fish aboard the *Cabrillo*. Exclaiming in French, dark eyes
sparkling with pleasure, Sarah Bernhardt ordered her catch, small
as it was, to be prepared for dinner.

It was May 19, 1906, and the farewell production of *Camille*
was scheduled for a few hours later at the ocean auditorium built
on the water at Venice, California. Sarah stayed, and fished, at the
hotel built like a ship, and she performed in the adjacent theater on
the wharf at the seaside resort, Venice of America. Having caught a
fish, Sarah wended her way to her quarters. Piled high in her dressing room were the results of a recent shopping trip to the Oriental
bazaar nearby: silk and crepe matinee coats of pink and pale blue
and mauve, all embroidered with butterflies and bamboo designs.

The tiny window in the dressing room provided a sparkling
view of the ocean, and the streaming sunshine picked out details

of the furnishings: a repoussé silver powder box, containers of pigment, eyebrow pencils, silver rouge pots, and scattered jewelry twinkling in the light. The tragedienne who attracted huge audiences wherever she went swooped up a small tan and white fox terrier, wriggling with joy at her return, and snuggled it close for a moment as she related the happy details of her fishing venture to a visiting reporter. Then she put down the small dog and closed her mind to the fun waiting outside the porthole.

Within moments Sarah became Marguerite Gautier, filled with the sadness and torment of the beautiful French courtesan in *Camille*, the play by Alexandre Dumas that became her signature role, performed all over the world more than three thousand times. Sarah's ability to sink fully into the character of the play made the tragic death scene so convincing that it became a trademark for "the Divine Sarah."

No one played tragedy with such believable intensity as Sarah Bernhardt, and no one brought as much passion and enthusiasm to the pursuit of pleasure. From fishing on the Southern California coast to bear hunting in the woods outside Seattle, on every western tour the French actress indulged in some kind of adventure. Sarah Bernhardt threw herself into life with the same characteristic energy she put into her stage appearances. Yet she often slept in a coffin, preparing for that final sleep.

She was born in Paris, France, on October 23, 1844, the illegitimate daughter of milliner-come-mistress Judith van Hard and, probably, law student Edouard Bernard. Named Henriette-Rosine Bernard, she was a thin, sickly child, alternately deeply depressed or shouting with joy. Her dramatic nature revealed itself early. At the age of eight, seeing her aunt's carriage stopped in the street near the house where her mother had left her for months and being forbidden to leave by her caretakers, she forced open a second-floor window and jumped out in front of the carriage. Although the fall resulted in a dislocated shoulder and shattered

Sarah Bernhardt

kneecap, her aunt was compelled to pay attention to the child's hysterical pleadings to be taken away.

Sarah could neither read nor write, and her behavior veered between opposite extremes of emotion, depending on her moods. The spectacular descent from the window achieved its goal: Her mother and her aunt decided something had to be done about her education. Her mother sent her to school, and later, with the help of the Duc de Morny, she was trained in dramatic arts and began her career at the Comédie-Française.

Always frail, she nearly died from lung problems, and as a teenager, sure that she would not live long, Sarah nagged her mother into buying her a coffin so that she could get used to lying in it; photographs show her in quiet repose within the silk-lined box. Yet her passionate energy was revealed in the many altercations with other actresses and producers that made her first years in theater so difficult.

By 1864 the aspiring actress had met with some success. Severely afflicted with stage fright, which affected her all her life, some of her performances were uneven at best. Reviews were not terrible, but for a young woman who expected perfection, even modest phrases like "she carries herself well and pronounces her words with perfect clarity" seemed the epitome of insult.

After performing a bad part in a poor play, Sarah went to Brussels, where she met Prince Henri de Ligne. An affair resulted in pregnancy, followed by the birth of a son, Maurice. Some fifteen years later, she still carried Maurice's first little shoes in her purse—they were once discovered by a customs inspector in the bottom of her handbag.

Sarah didn't speak English, but that had not deterred British audiences from growing hysterical over her command of a tragic role. Her flamboyant lifestyle added to the reputation that carried her to triumph across the Channel. Reports of her menagerie, including a lion; pictures of the opulent interior of her home; her jewels; her lovers; and the coffin in which she still sometimes slept all fanned the imagination of the staid British public.

Her fame was immense in Europe by the time she first toured the United States in 1880. After early appearances in eastern states, where her adventures made headlines and huge crowds waited for a glimpse of the famous face and form, she started west, playing in major cities like Salt Lake, Denver, and, finally, San Francisco. San Francisco's *Morning Call* of May 17, 1887, described the well-dressed throng that turned out for her first performance:

> *When 8 o'clock arrived and the house was filled it was, in the words of the old-time usher "Gus," the best house the Baldwin has seen. Bob Eberle ran his arithmetical eye over the assemblage and put it down at over $4500. The ladies costumes were of the most elaborate order, even to the family circle, usually staid, but for this occasion brilliant in the sheen of silks and the glitter of diamonds.*

The reviewer found not one wrong note in Bernhardt's appearance at the Baldwin Theater. In the May 30, 1887, edition of the paper, an accounting provided total receipts from her performances at nearly $41,400. Reporters found her exploits off the stage as compelling to write about as the tragedies she enacted.

Within a few years, Sarah's extremely thin figure had been caricatured in Europe and America. Drawings of the actress in newspapers show a wraith figure crowned by a large head and masses of wild hair. The *Call* of April 1891 provided a full description of the famous actress and her lifestyle: "In the Salon of 1876 Bernhardt's portrait was twice exhibited. One of the pictures shows her sitting in a white gown, slightly reclining on a sofa, and at her feet lays an immense dog. When Alexandre Dumas saw this portrait he remarked: 'Un chien qui garde un os'; in English: 'A dog watching a bone.'"

Despite the death's-head images that marked her fame, Sarah lived every moment with total intensity. The same reviewer in the

*Call* described her frail constitution: "which does not, at the same time, prevent her from drawing largely on all the sources of enjoyment in life. She rides spirited horses and drives a fiery Russian span."

Finally, says the admiring reporter, she is "passionately fond" of fencing, which she learned in order to play a role that required she masquerade as a boy. That role may have been one of the most difficult she ever performed. In fact, without Sarah in the lead, Alfred de Musset's drama *Lorenzaccio* might not have been produced, because it was considered too difficult to stage. It was based on a story from the dreaded Medici reign in Florence, Italy. In the play, Sarah's role was that of the young Lorenzo, intent on ridding the city of the tyrant Alexander. As a correspondent in the *Argonaut* of 1897 wrote,

> *She is the incarnation of the voluptuous, cynical, tigerish Foul Lorenzo. Every expression of face is a study. She has learned to walk, move, and speak like a man. Not once does she betray her sex. In the fencing scene with Scoronconcocto, when the fury of hate and vengeance is upon the youth and he presses the bravo, half forgetful that it is not his abhorred enemy he holds at the point of his sword, Sarah is superb. It appears that at every rehearsal she donned male attire, that she might grow thoroughly accustomed to it, and the result is that she is as much at home in doublet and hose as if she had never worn a skirt in her life.*

On the first night of the play, the *Argonaut* correspondent reported that the audience "reached delirium point." The review continued, "I shall not soon forget the appearance of the house, the sound of the applause still rings in my ears, and I shall long be haunted by the vision of the panther-like form, mastered by the demon of murder, as it sprang on its sleeping victim."

At this time Sarah was fifty-two years old, yet no one considered her too old to take the lead in any play, even one so demanding as *Lorenzaccio*. Nor had her energy diminished: While she rehearsed the fencing scenes during the day, she performed every night in the original French version of *Camille*, even acting as stage manager between times.

The ability to convince her audiences that she was the person she represented in the role she played was made abundantly clear when she played Joan of Arc in her sixties. At one point in the play Joan was asked her age by a judge. "Nineteen," Sarah would say, turning slightly toward the audience, which, knowing the truth, sometimes stood up and cheered her ability to convince them of her youth.

A description of her appearance just after the turn of the century belies the skeleton caricature so long used to identify the actress. A reporter described the lines scribed by time and suffering in the famous countenance:

> *Sarah Bernhardt is not precisely beautiful. She has deeply expressive blue eyes, white, even teeth, a fine nose whose nostrils nervously tremble in passion, and a purely chiseled chin. The best gift nature has bestowed upon her is her voice. This soft, deep organ is capable of unlimited modulation; its tones creep into the soul of the audience, and vaguely suggest a sultry evening breeze, or a warm, heavy fragrance of pinks. When she is on the stage her voice dominates the conversation as an organ does a church service.*

Members of the clergy, on the other hand, were not so admiring of Sarah's performances. Bishops and ministers warned their flocks away from the dramas that she brought to life. The California editor of the *Wave* in 1891 defended her, however, explaining,

> *It is not the fault of this woman that there is in the characters she represents—however baleful and obnoxious they may be—more dramatic value than in the village maiden. The genius of Bernhardt rarely makes the woman she represents loveable to those who see the representations; her La Tosca is a tigress, her Cleopatra a serpent, and her*

Sarah Bernhardt, left, holding paper, performing in *L'Aiglon*

*Camille a cat. As she portrays them we pity them for their
sufferings, but abhor them for their deeds.*

Sarah had a hard time understanding the objections to the
characters in plays such as *Camille*, which she performed repeatedly
in America. "This play, that the public rushed to see in crowds,
shocked the overstrained Puritanism of the small American states,"
she wrote. "The critics of the large cities discussed this modern
Magdalene. But those of the small towns began by throwing
stones at her. This stilted reserve on the part of the public, preju-
diced against Marguerite Gautier, we met from time to time in
the small cities." For Sarah a town of thirty thousand was "small."

"*Quand meme*" was Sarah's motto. The phrase means roughly
"in spite of everything," and it perfectly described her feisty nature.
She adopted the motto at the age of nine after accepting a dare
to jump a ditch, which resulted in a fall and a sprained wrist. She
insisted she would do it again if dared. If nothing else in her long,
adventurous life, she always dared.

While on her first tour of America, she went to the manufacturer and bought a Colt revolver. This was not an empty gesture
designed for publicity. When an attempt was made to rob her train
of the jewels and money it was said to contain, her "pretty little
revolver" ornamented with cat's-eye stones did not have to be
used, as a guard apprehended the thief. Sarah's revolver was not,
however, just an unusual accessory. She was a good shot. While in
Seattle she went on a bear hunt and returned without a bear, but
instead she carried a gray squirrel and several birds.

Traveling in a special "Palace Car," she crisscrossed America
many times. In one season she made 156 appearances in fifty cities and towns. The luxurious railcar was embellished with walls of
inlaid wood, lit by brass gas lamps and furnished with splendid car-
pets, sofas, a piano, and potted palms. Ten people could be seated
at the dining table, and two chefs prepared meals.

Her tour up the coast of California in 1906 avoided San Francisco, still cooling after the earthquake that had destroyed so much of the famed city just a few days earlier. Instead she played for seven thousand people at the Greek Theatre across the Bay at Berkeley. The interview published by *The Theater Magazine* the following month delved deeply into Sarah's preparation for her roles. "I read the piece through, and yes, the interpretation of the character I am to play comes to me at once when first I read over the play," she replied in answer to a question. "I see it as it is to be done at once. If I cannot feel the part," and here, says the interviewer, she pressed her jeweled hands to her heart, "I reject the play. I know instantly. If I do not catch the feeling I will not touch the piece."

Except in California, her 1906 tour of the West was complicated by a syndicate of theater owners who refused to book her into their houses for economic reasons: Whichever theater signed Bernhardt got all the crowds, while the other houses stood empty. Always aided by clever managers, Sarah instead played in whatever hall was available, including tents, all across the Southwest. Such was her fame by then that, it's said, a Texas cowboy demanded entrance at six-gun point to a sold-out house; inside he asked what this French "gal" did—sing or dance?

Farther north, in Butte, Montana, Sarah played in a huge, unheated roller-skating rink. Fewer than twelve hundred people bought tickets. Canceling the appearance was discussed, but Sarah insisted the show go on, even though there would be no profits. The *Anaconda Standard* of May 6, 1906, noted that the Holland rink was freezing, the actors appeared in furs, and the people in the audience were wrapped up against the cold. As if that were not enough to discourage even the hardiest drama lover, "halfway down the hall not a sound from the stage could be heard," said the *Standard*. Still, at the end of the final act, "The freezing audience was as enthusiastic and warm as it could be, and the great actress was called before the stage repeatedly."

It was her only appearance that year in Montana. The *Standard* continued, "Mme. Bernhardt's farewell appearance in Butte was under extreme difficulties, but there are at least a thousand people who are glad they had the privilege and opportunity to see her again and once more sit under the spell of her genius."

A captive audience in 1913 sat rapt as she read for two thousand inmates at San Quentin prison. Between engagements in San Francisco, Sarah performed her son's play, *Une Nuit de Noel sous la Terreur* (A Christmas Night under the Terror). It concluded with prisoners being released from the infamous French prison, the Bastille. Played in the prison yard crowded with men standing in striped uniforms, Sarah enthralled her audience. A letter from the prisoners thanked her for an hour's "perfect liberty" despite the high walls and the treacherous waters that kept the inmates confined.

Ever ready for adventure, during that same visit Sarah flew out over the Bay in a two-seater aircraft that promised the ultimate in freedom.

Two years later Sarah's own independence was threatened. She had suffered intermittently for years from a series of injuries to her right knee. The most disabling had occurred in Rio de Janeiro in October 1905. During the last act of *La Tosca*, she was required to fling herself from the parapet of a prison. Mattresses to cushion the fall on the other side had been misplaced, and Sarah landed hard on the already weak right knee. She declined treatment in South America and departed for New York. She couldn't walk for weeks but resumed her American tour in November, playing sixty-two cities.

The damaged knee never healed properly. Later, walking became so painful that sets were rearranged to provide support as she crossed the stage. By 1915 gangrene had set in, and Sarah, then seventy-one and suffering from chronic uremia, insisted the leg be amputated. Doctors declined until she threatened to shoot herself in the knee if they didn't do as she asked. Finally one surgeon agreed. She reportedly went under the knife singing the French national anthem, "La Marseillaise."

Disliking the prosthetic device that would allow her to be somewhat mobile, the woman known for her sinuous grace and feline movements continued playing scenes from the roles she'd made famous, but she stayed in one place to do it. Sitting, reclining on a couch, or standing beside a prop, she used her voice, her hands, and all the intensity she could command to carry her audience away. Refusing the indignity of a wheelchair, she had a special litter chair built, complete with gilded carvings, in which she was carried about like royalty.

Despite her missing limb she visited troops near Verdun, not far from the front lines where soldiers were engaged in bloody battles of World War I. Performing in whatever accommodation she could find—from mess tents to barns—she recited patriotic pieces for the French troopers who rose in waves to cheer their one-legged goddess. She returned to America in 1916 to recoup her fortunes, but a year later she spent four months sidelined by kidney problems that required surgery.

Despite changes in theatrical tastes, Sarah Bernhardt never retired. Vaudeville was not too low for "the Divine Sarah." Instead of performing complete plays, she reprised scenes she'd made famous. The shorter format fit the customary vaudeville bill, which included everything from trained-animal acts to black-face minstrels. Unable to use the gestures and sinuous postures that were so much a part of her fame, she relied on her masterful voice, moments of silence, or a single lift of the hand to convey her meaning, and audiences responded deliriously.

Sarah was also seen on the silent screen. Her first cinema appearance was at the Paris Exposition in 1900. By then she was sixty-six years old, yet her interest in the new medium continued until her death in 1923. She made eight films. Her biggest hit was

*Queen Elizabeth*, and she was shooting a film on location when she collapsed. She died on March 26, in the arms of her son Maurice. That evening, theaters in Paris paid silent homage for two minutes. She was buried in the rosewood coffin her mother had purchased at her insistence when she was but fifteen years old, sure that her life would be tragically short.

# Lillian Russell

## The American Beauty

*If a woman gets the reputation of being a professional beauty, it*
*is hard work to live up to it.*

—Lillian Russell, *The Theatre*
*Magazine,* 1905

The green silk robe shimmered in the light of the dressing
room. Adjusting the neckline, Lillian Russell glanced into the
mirror and considered the interviewer's question about beauties
never appreciating their good looks. "I think they do," she countered. "They are glad to have it, as they are grateful for any other
gift. I am pleased and gratified when someone says I look nice."

Looking "nice" was a part of the job that the corn-fed beauty
from America's heartland never forgot. The costume she wore in
the second act of *Lady Teazle* showed off her abundant charms to
perfection. The green silk, the large plumed hat, and the ebony
walking stick adorned with orange ribbons were but a pretty frame
for the statuesque blond performer whose sumptuous exterior
diverted attention from a sharp mind and a warm heart.

As she continued dressing for the second act of the play, she
answered questions from Miss Ada Patterson, longtime reporter
for *The Theatre Magazine.* How, asked Patterson, had a girl from
Iowa earned the name "America's Beauty"?

"I came away from Clinton when I was six months old,
and I don't remember much about it," she told the reporter. A
backward glance over a smooth white shoulder gave a glimpse of

the famous smile, curving perfect lips. A spark of mischief flashed in the beautiful, blue eyes framed by long, thick eyelashes as she added, "Although there are Tabbies who say they remember my life there when I was six months old sixty years ago."

The feature later published in *The Theatre Magazine* of February 1905 never came right out and said that America's most famous beauty was now forty-three years old. Behind her lay phenomenal success as well as heartbreak and failure, yet none of it dimmed the glow. The interviewer that day compared the throat and shoulders rising from the green silk to the *Venus de Milo*. The pure soprano voice still hit high C with ease, and, after more than twenty-three years on stage, the name Lillian Russell still drew people to the theater.

Lillian Russell's thoughts on beauty were read avidly by women all over America when Ada Patterson's interview appeared. The reporter described how the girl christened Helen Louise Leonard demonstrated the proper placement of an enormous hat atop a cluster of golden curls. Adjusting the tilted brim, the star gently lectured the reporter about her theories on good looks. "But what is beauty? It is nothing compared to intelligence and a manner. Meet a woman who has intelligence and a beautiful manner, and who stops to think whether she is beautiful or not?"

One set of admirers could testify to the gracious manner, warm heart, and generosity of the star named Lillian Russell. She was notoriously kind to people who worked for her, even when they stole from her, as one did. Yet another group that she did business with, theater producers and promoters, knew they were dealing with a hard-driving woman who understood exactly what she was worth and made them pay her price. It was her voice, her looks, and her reputation that could ask for, and receive, huge sums for appearances on stage even when beautiful, talented, younger women contested her reign.

From her earliest years, Helen Louise Leonard had the kind of beauty that stopped traffic. She had a voice that her mother, Cynthia Rowland Leonard, an ardent feminist, paid to have trained when her fifth daughter was still in her teens. Helen Louise was educated at the Convent of the Sacred Heart in Chicago and attended finishing school at Park Institute. She took singing lessons and sang in the church choir at the Episcopal Church. She was the apple of her father Charlie's eye, his "airy, fairy Nellie," the youngest daughter with the looks and the voice of an angel.

Her parents separated when she was in her teens, and her mother took Helen Louise and moved to New York, where young Helen started training for grand opera. She could sustain the highest notes with virtually no effort, and do it again and again without strain. Her voice coach, Dr. Leopold Damrosch, told her mother that with a few years of training he could make her a diva to rival the best.

The beautiful blond from Iowa had other ideas. Years of training and rehearsals, with only bit parts and backup roles as an understudy, lay before her on the road to stardom in opera. Helen Louise ignored her mother's plans and made her own career choice by secretly joining the Park Theater Company in Brooklyn. She was eighteen when she danced onstage for the first time in the chorus of *H. M. S. Pinafore*, a Gilbert and Sullivan operetta that went on to resounding success. A neighbor of Cynthia Leonard told her about a young woman who resembled her daughter appearing in the new play he'd seen. The secret came out when her mother, fuming, rose from a seat in the audience and shouted out, "That's my Nell!"

Cynthia and her daughter were often at odds. "Mothers are good for an actress to have near until they are sixteen," Lillian later said, "and after that they are apt to be a nuisance."

Her feminist mother thought a career in light opera was beneath her daughter, but the principles of independence she'd

Portrait of Lillian Russell as *The Grand Duchess* from the play of the same name

taught had obviously found fertile ground. Eager to dive into this new life that had opened before her, not only did Helen Louise continue onstage, she took a fateful step that nearly sundered her relationship with her mother. She accepted a proposal of marriage shortly before the end of *Pinafore*'s run in 1879.

Although a handsome millionaire was courting her, she married the company's musical director, Harry Braham. That marked the end of her appearance in the chorus. She withdrew from the company and settled into domestic life, a life she was born for, according to her friend, actress Marie Dressler.

Soon Helen Louise was pregnant, and a baby son was born. Despite Dressler's opinion about Helen's natural domestic tendencies, a nurse was hired to care for the baby so that the actress could once again take up her career. Her paycheck made a big difference for the little family. Her much older husband was not happy with that decision, but a woman raised to be independent was not easily swayed when fame and fortune called.

Then one day she returned to find her baby desperately ill. Despite all attempts to cure the infant, he died in convulsions. Apparently the inexperienced nurse had accidentally pierced his abdomen with a diaper pin. Harry Braham accused his wife of neglect.

Grieving over the death of her son, feeling betrayed by her husband's accusations, and beset by her mother's vitriolic accusations against Braham, Helen concentrated on her career. Tony Pastor, legendary producer of musical comedy, heard her sing at the home of a friend and, consequently, offered her a job. Her mother argued for a return to the career path she'd planned for her daughter in grand opera, but Helen Louise liked the immediate success she'd already tasted in comic opera. At nineteen, with a statuesque figure, golden curls, skin like "roses and cream," and a soprano voice that could do everything with ease, she had found her first mentor in Tony Pastor.

Pastor's theater specialized in send-ups of popular plays like *The Pirates of Penzance*, produced by Pastor as *The Pie Rats of Penn-Yann*. The impresario thought Helen Louise Leonard too dowdy and provincial a name for the gorgeous blond with the voice of an angel. In 1880 Pastor presented her as "Lillian Russell, the English Ballad Singer." She chose the two names from a list, later saying she liked the way the name began and ended with the same letter. Pastor gave her parts that showed off her talents. She was a rousing success, so much so that Pastor feared she would be spoiled by adulation. Instead of continuing to build her reputation in New York, he sent her west with Willie Edouin's touring company. As she traveled by rail toward the Pacific Ocean, she learned to play poker and pinochle.

In San Francisco Lillian Russell became the toast of the town. The City by the Bay was bubbling over with brash enterprise, fueled by newly made fortunes dug from the golden hills. The troupe that played *Babes in the Woods* and *Fun in a Photograph Gallery* earned recognition in the newspapers, and reporters took note of the fresh, young singer who made several appearances: "There is a pretty young girl, a Miss Lillian Russell, who has a voice as sweet and fresh as a thrush, but Miss Russell sings everything too fast and loses half the effect she might give."

The same review in the *Argonaut* took note of her costumes, reporting that they were very pretty, pale-blue satin painted with poppies and hat to match, a paler blue satin with trailing vines and morning glories, and another hat to match, and a pretty affair of pink-and-white and swansdown. Unfortunately financial disaster stalked Willie Edouin's troupe, which even the newspapers noted. Said one supporter: "Willie Edouin has been struggling manfully against small business at the Standard. He has one of the cleverest companies I have seen here. The report took note of Edouin's newest performer: And pretty Miss Lillian Russell, who is Mrs. Braham in private, has a mezzo soprano voice of beautiful quality and immense promise."

The promise of financial reward did not pay out. The *San Francisco Call* noted: "The performances of this company have been, in many instances, exceptionally clever, and, only, because of the presence in our city of several combinations presenting similar entertainments, can their partial failure be accounted for."

The troupe left the city with nearly empty pockets, and in Colorado illness caused a cancellation of performances. Broke, the company dissolved, but Edouin and his wife chaperoned the young actress home.

In October 1881, Lillian Russell was back playing at New York's Bijou Opera House, a somewhat seasoned twenty-year-old performer who had no trouble in performance but had not yet learned the business side of the entertainment business. She'd seen how easily the money disappeared despite good reviews and a strong company. Fresh from the financial disaster in the West, her inexperience in the trade led her astray. Faced with a number of offers upon her return to New York, she found she could not say no.

Early in 1882 she signed conflicting contracts with rival companies and, threatened with litigation when all was revealed, escaped by sailing for England. While the press at home called her reckless and unsavory, her debut at London's Gaiety Theatre set her star ablaze.

Once again, her romantic inclinations betrayed her. She and Braham had divorced after the death of their baby, but she still had a soft spot for the boys in the band. In May 1884 she married, and again it was to a musician, English composer Edward Solomon. By the winter of the following year, Lillian, her husband, and their baby daughter Dorothy had returned to New York.

Reality slapped the face of the famous beauty once more. In England a woman named Jane Isaacs Solomon filed suit against her husband—for bigamy. Edward was arrested in England, and Lillian's hopes for a happy married life were shattered. She announced she would seek an annulment. Although she concealed the pain of Solomon's betrayal, the gorgeous petals of America's Beauty were tarnished by scandal. Even scandal, however, brought people to a theater.

Lillian decided to make another tour of the American West, and this one turned out to be much more successful. She signed with the J. C. Duff Company and embarked on a long tour of cities along the Pacific Coast. At the end of two seasons on the road, Lillian was a bigger star than ever, and, as she entered her thirties, she, herself, was bigger than ever. The hourglass figure that had contributed to her fame now required the tight cinching of a strong corset. Lillian, who reportedly could eat a dozen ears of corn as an appetizer, fully enjoyed the offerings of the best restaurants. Knowing her beauty was a huge part of her success, she began to exercise religiously. She became a fanatical bicyclist, and her friend, millionaire railroad salesman Diamond Jim Brady, presented her with a gold-plated bicycle.

Always questioned about her beauty secrets, Lillian recommended vigorous exercise at a time when the myth of women as the "weaker sex" was accepted without question. Lillian's advice flew in the face of convention. "Bicycle riding to women usually means peddling along dismounting every five or ten minutes, but this will not do at all if you mean to reduce your weight," she warned. In addition, and to the horror of those who already considered bicycles for women a tool of the devil, Lillian advised against wearing a corset while exercising. "Every muscle must be unhampered," she insisted.

She also loosened the corset when she sat down to a feast with Diamond Jim. The legendary railroad equipment salesman had made, and spent, millions of dollars, and a lot of his profits went into huge dinner parties for himself and his friends. Lillian reportedly matched him at the table but handily outdid him at maintaining her weight. She once took off nearly thirty pounds and reduced her waist from twenty-seven to twenty-two inches by sticking to a schedule of exercise that included bicycle riding, tennis, and workouts in a gymnasium; Turkish baths; and massage.

According to the June 25, 1922, edition of the *Ogden Standard Examiner*,

> *Lillian Russell made no secret of some of the measures and means she employed to retain her extraordinary good looks, but she did not tell the whole story. She did not say that in addition to the bats, cold creams, cosmetics, exercise and wholesome living she also made liberal use of common sense, self-control, persistence, energy and cheerfulness—factors neglected by many women who faithfully follow her other formulas.*
>
> *She loved Broadway's sensuous pleasures, the bright lights, the lilting music, the fragrance of flowers, the dainties of the table, but she had the strength of character to sacrifice those pleasures that might injure her voice or physical charms. She adopted rules of health which she observed religiously until they became a part of her life.*
>
> *One of those rules was to get sufficient sleep. She did not pin herself down to certain hours or a certain number of hours. She knew that nature demands a certain amount of sleep to repair completely the waste of tissue that goes on during the waking hours, a person doing no mental or physical work needs very little sleep. Mental or physical labor needs enough sleep for complete reparation and the amount depends partly upon the amount of waste and partly upon rapidity of repair.*
>
> *During youth repair goes on much more rapidly than in later life and as the waste is much greater in later life the older one grows, the more sleep he requires if he does not cut down the amount of his work. Lillian insists that insufficient sleep means insufficient repair and a longing for more sleep to make up the deficiency. When a person has had enough sleep to complete the repair process the person awakens naturally.*
>
> *Lillian did not regulate her sleep by the clock but let nature regulate the amount she needed. When she awoke she was completely refreshed, her mind was clear and re-*

*ceptive, and she could learn her lines with but little effort. There was never the dark circles under the eyes, the dull eyes, the strained expression that comes from insufficient sleep.*

*In the matter of food and drink she was as careful as in other habits of life. She had seen many a girl's face become bloated, blotchy, and pimply, many a figure become course, many a voice become husky and many a constitution wrecked after too many midnight suppers. So she had the good sense to draw the line at excesses in food and drink. She knew that a single night's carousing would have such a disastrous effect upon her complexion that it would take several days work to restore it to its ante-prandial conditions, and she had the will power to resist temptation.*

In 1907 Lillian was once again on tour in her private Pullman car. Her play, *Wildfire*, was a huge success. According to an enthusiastic report in the *Anaconda* (Montana) *Standard*: "Miss Lillian Russell, the celebrated actress and American beauty, is making her first visit to Butte. Miss Russell's public interviews and writings have long been noted for the good advice to young women, based on her own extended and varied experiences and observations."

Lillian's recommendations about religion were also quoted extensively. "I am to a certain extent a believer in Christian Science. Mrs. [Mary Baker] Eddy's teachings are not new, however. Much of her arguments were taken from the Confessions of Marcus Aurelius. She has read Buddha, and dipped into the writings of Confucius. Her doctrines contain the best teachings of those ancient wise men," Lillian expounded, somewhat to the surprise of the *Standard* interviewer.

Marriage and divorce were also covered, with the star using the newspaper to advance some rather radical ideas for the time. "Marriage is not an ideal institution as it is," she said. "The idea that as soon as a man marries you that he should assume the airs of a proprietor and tell a woman where she should go and whom

Lillian Russell

she should meet and why, especially if she is a woman of feeling, is irksome."

*Irksome* was too mild a word for Lillian's third marriage. In 1894 she wed a singer, John Haley Augustin Chatterton, who styled himself Signor Giovanni Perugini. Her actress friend, Marie Dressler, portrayed the tenor as a conceited buffoon who stooped to embarrassing Lillian onstage. After several months of discord, Lillian kicked him out. Disillusioned, she threw herself into her career, taking a hand in management of her company. Although her appearance in *The Goddess of Truth* and other productions under the direction of Henry E. Abby were not well received, she made a comeback in *An American Beauty* and thus acquired her nickname.

In 1899 Lillian joined Weber and Fields Music Hall, where she earned more than twelve hundred dollars a week. Until 1904, when Joe Weber and Lew Fields dissolved their partnership, she enjoyed a fizzy success in comic opera. *Lady Teazle*, a musical version of *The School for Scandal*, showcased her talents as an actress. Minor surgery on her throat had not helped her deteriorating voice, so she began playing exclusively comic roles. She covered thousands of miles in her private railroad car to indifferent success and finally returned to vaudeville and a popular reprise of some of her most famous songs.

Still beautiful, fiercely intelligent, and as opinionated as her mother ever had been, Lillian began writing a syndicated newspaper column, lectured on health and beauty and love, supported the vote for women, and put out a line of cosmetics called Lillian Russell's Own Preparation.

In 1912 she married Alexander Pollock Moore, owner of the *Pittsburgh Leader*. Moore was everything her musician husbands had not been, and his power in conservative politics matched her interests well. She recruited for the Marine Corps and supported War Bond drives during the First World War and afterward raised money for the American Legion.

She made a movie version of *Wildfire* in 1914, starring with John Barrymore, but the movie was not particularly successful. Her public appearances, however, especially when she closed with her song "Come Down My Evenin' Star," still roused huge enthusiasm. Her profile, which was as well-known as her name, was featured on cigar bands and matchbox covers, theater posters, and magazine covers. The *Illustrated American* declared: "There are those of course, who have preferences in other directions when it comes to female beauty. They may prefer theirs darker, or slighter, or more willowy, or shorter or taller. But any such predilection is a personal matter, after all everyone acknowledges Miss Russell a beauty and a rare one at that."

Lillian always knew her beauty was an asset, but after her work for equal rights for women, for political causes, and on behalf of American servicemen, she decided to enter the political arena herself, and, in 1915, she declared her candidacy for mayor of New York. The woman whose first tour of the West had ended in economic failure had learned a lot about the world of commerce, and her candidacy was founded on the principles of sound business practice. "The reason I want to vote is because I pay three kinds of taxes—on my property, my income and my business—and I think I ought to have something to say about what to do with my money," she told the *New York Herald*.

Women did not receive the national right to vote until 1920, and Lillian's run for mayor did not succeed, except that it gave her another avenue to express the strong beliefs she had in equal rights. Despite her age, her good looks still engaged the largely male press. One editor noted that "if perennial beauty is an outward manifestation of inward spiritual grace, then New York's government should be crowned with success under her hand."

She campaigned vigorously for Warren G. Harding for president; as a result, in 1922 President Harding appointed her as a special investigator on immigration. During a tour of Europe in this capacity, she sustained a bad fall and, despite the injuries, turned in her report urging restrictions on immigration. The fall occurred while she was onboard the ship that was returning to America from London. Lillian was violently thrown to the deck of the vessel during a storm. Shortly after she made it home in Pittsburgh, she collapsed from complications attributed to the fall.

In addition to her husband, her daughter, niece, and her two sisters were present at her bedside during her last moments on Earth. The superstar of the "Gay Nineties," died at her Pittsburgh home on June 7, 1922, of "cardiac exhaustion."

According to the June 17, 1922, edition of the *Oneonta Daily Star*, a bodyguard of US marines accompanied her body from the Trinity Protestant Episcopal Church, where her funeral was held to the cemetery. A detachment from the American Legion post, of which Lillian was a member, formed the firing squad at her last resting place. Her body was placed in a vault until her husband could erect a suitable mausoleum.

Among those who attended the funeral was the secretary of labor, representatives of the Actor's Equity Association and the National Vaudeville Association, and senators from California, New York, and Colorado. Lillian had expressed the wish that no flowers be sent at the time of her death, believing, she said, that people in moderate circumstances should not feel the necessity of contributing.

# Helena Modjeska

## The Polish Phenomenon

*"The sorcery of a genius superb in power and marvelous in grace was upon them."*

—*Territorial Enterprise*, Virginia City,
Nevada, October 23, 1877

A cold wind blew down the canyon, carrying pellets of frozen snow and grit from the mines in the hills surrounding Virginia City, Nevada. The wind swirled through the narrow streets, bringing damp, cold air and the smell of wood smoke into National Guard Hall. A restless audience debated the prospects of entertainment this stormy evening. Could a Polish woman really deliver the goods tonight?

Miners with callused hands mingled with clean-fingered merchants and discussed the probabilities of a rousing performance. Gamblers watched the stage for signs that the mysterious Madam Modjeska would soon appear and wagered she would be unintelligible in the French play *Adrienne Lecouvreur*. Helena Modjeska barely spoke English, they said with knowing looks. Her English teacher had been German, they chuckled, so the odds were good that the great tragedy would become a farce.

Backstage, Helena Modjeska paced the boards, running her lines and tamping down nerves. She was more than six thousand miles from Cracow, waiting in the wings to perform a play in front of an audience of Comstock miners about a Parisian courtesan who had died nearly fifty years before. This brawling town of Virginia

City was shocking, with its gambling dens and brothels doing brisk business alongside shops, hotels, and, just one street away, churches. How could she possibly convey the pathos and strength of the character through two language barriers in a town described as an outpost of hell?

That she did so, and with startling success, was chronicled in the Nevada press. Barely two weeks after Helena's thirty-seventh birthday, the *Territorial Enterprise* of October 23, 1877, presented her with a gift of unstinting praise:

> *The acting of Madame Modjeska last night at National Guard Hall was not like anything ever seen before in Virginia City. It was the perfect realization of something which we fancy is dreamed of by us all, but which we have waited and waited for through the years until deep down in our hearts we have concluded it was something too rare for any earthly one to give realization to—that it was but a longing of the divine within us which only in some other state less sordid, dull and cold that this could find full expression. But last night the dream was made real, and more than once did the audience rub their eyes and look up with that questioning gaze which men put on when startled suddenly from a broken sleep.*

Barely two months from her debut on the California stage, Helena Modjeska had proven she could hold an American audience in the palm of her hand as well as she held the audiences she'd charmed in Europe. It proved, in a way, that she had made the right decision in leaving Cracow and the fame she had earned there. In only one year she had succeeded, despite launching her career for a second time in a strange land where even simple conversation with her neighbors was nearly impossible.

Helena Modjeska had conquered adversity more than once in her life. She was born October 12, 1840, and named Jadwiga Opid by her mother, Josephine Benda, who had been widowed five years before. She was the first of two daughters born several years after

Josephine's husband had died, leaving their three legitimate sons fatherless. The family guardian was a schoolteacher, Michael Opid, whose name was given to Helena and her little sister. Opid had an interest in music and drama. Helena grew up with fond memories of him and his lively manner and wide-ranging interests. She had barely hit her teens when Opid died, and the loss of property and income once again left her mother in dire financial straits.

Helena went to a convent school but yearned for a more creative life on the stage. With the blessings and help of a wealthy friend of her mother, Gustav Sinnmayer, Helena dropped out of school and began taking acting lessons.

She was eighteen years old when she and Sinnmayer left Cracow for a small town fifty miles to the east that was famed for its salt mines. At a charity fair there, she made her theatrical debut.

Then, on January 27, 1861, Helena gave birth to a son. Sinnmayer, twenty years Helena's senior, fathered the child. "He had already become as dear to me as my own brothers," she wrote in her memoirs, "and besides, my imagination adorned him with the attributes of all the impossible heroes I read about in poetry or prose."

It isn't clear whether she and Sinnmayer had married, although she implies they had in her memoirs. Sinnmayer had taken the name *Modrzejewski*, also *Modjeski*, which Helena later used in its feminine form, *Modjeska*, in France and America.

She later gave birth to a second child, a daughter, but her interest in a career on the stage did not wane as the demands of motherhood increased. Soon Sinnmayer gathered a troupe of actors, including some of Helena's siblings. They were very popular on tour in neighboring towns, but once again tragedy cast a pall on success.

"They say misfortunes never come singly, but are accompanied by other misfortunes, forming a long linked chain," Helena wrote. "Blow after blow struck my heart and bruised it to the core."

Helena's three-year-old daughter, Marylka, died. Sunk in grief, Helena became ill. Adding to the mental and emotional burden, her family urged her to leave Sinnmayer. Without clearly explaining the reasons behind the separation, Helena returned to Cracow with her son Rudolph, but without Sinnmayer. With the help of relatives and friends, she was soon starring in productions at Cracow theaters. Ambitious and talented, she set her sights on the Warsaw stage.

Her passionate nature, however, led her to challenge the regime that controlled Poland. Rebelling against the political situation, Helena became popular in nationalistic plays that drew the ire of censors. Despite the danger of reprisal from tweaking the nose of authority, she continued voicing political opposition through the parts she played. Her skills and her popularity increased, but she dreamed of greater triumphs. In 1866 she left Warsaw behind, headed for Paris.

There she met a young Polish aristocrat who helped her career. Count Karol Bozenta Chlapowski, another rebel, had recently been freed from a Prussian prison where he had been confined more than a year for engaging in revolutionary activities. Helena and Count Bozenta were kindred spirits, with strong nationalistic beliefs. They were married in 1868, and Chlapowski directed Helena's career to a pinnacle in Europe. She was earning the highest salary of any performer and was offered a life engagement at the Imperial Theatre in Warsaw.

So what was she doing in 1877 on a drafty stage in National Guard Hall in the barren hills of Nevada? Why would she leave behind assured success in the cosmopolitan cities of Europe for a risky life in the rugged mining camps of the American West?

She came to participate in the American dream of freedom and, more specifically, to live the ideal of a pastoral life in golden California. "I pictured myself a life of toil under the blue skies of California, among the hills, riding on horseback with a gun over

Helena Modjeska
LIBRARY OF CONGRESS

my shoulder, [sic] I imagined all sorts of things except what was really in store for me."

The idea of peace, freedom, and happiness was a welcome change from the intense labors of the actress who was often under close watch by the secret police. During seven years in Poland, she had learned and performed 284 roles in several languages created by a variety of playwrights from Shakespeare to Goethe, as well as works from Polish dramatists. She was the center of a glittering social circle that included the leading artistic and intellectual talents of the day.

Unfortunately her work, her social life, and worrying about the police surveillance on her husband weakened her physically and emotionally. She caught typhoid fever. Recovery was slow, but during quiet evenings at home she listened to the glowing ideas of an American utopia developed by her husband and his friend, author Henryk Sienkiewicz. In later years Sienkiewicz became a noted literary figure, most famous for writing *Quo Vadis?* but also well-known for penning short stories based on his experiences in California.

A noble dream was conceived among the members of Helena's inner circle—that of a California farm that would house and support a colony of Polish emigrants. In her memoirs Helena says she considered the winter evening in 1875 that led to the American adventure "a stroke of fate." She half listened while the group of friends who had gathered at her home talked, admitting she was in a "torpid state" until the conversation turned to America.

> *Someone brought news of the coming Centennial Exposition in America. Sienkiewicz, with his vivid imagination, described the unknown country in the most attractive terms. Maps were brought out and California discussed. It was worthwhile to hear the young men's various opinions about the Gold West: "You cannot die of hunger there, that is quite sure!" said one. "Rabbits, hares and partridges are unguarded! You have only to go out and shoot them!"*

Helena's husband proposed a six-month vacation, chiefly to benefit his wife's health, but the others were intent on establishing their utopian colony. The legends of California's bounty influenced the group. Stories were told of travelers' claims about the far-off land where "the fruit of the cactus grow [sic] wild, and they say the latter is simply delicious." The lure of a land free from war and oppression, a paradise of orange groves and abundant game, of perfect weather and untrammeled freedom coalesced into a definite plan. The die was cast, and strife-torn Poland was left behind.

In July 1876, the eight-member nucleus of the colony landed in New York and then traveled to the farm near Anaheim in Southern California, where Sienkiewicz had scouted suitable property. He had gone ahead to prepare for the expatriate band's arrival at the farm he had purchased.

Unfortunately the dream of a bountiful future failed within a year. The men of the colony were unused to working as common laborers, and their utopian dream began to crumble. By the end of the year, Helena and her husband were feeling the financial pinch. She sold her silverware to raise money and left for San Francisco in the hope of reviving her career; her aristocratic husband and their son stayed behind, living in a rustic shack in the Santa Ana hills, cooking over an open fire.

As the property was being auctioned in early 1877, Helena discovered the difficulties in gaining the attention of theater managers. Despite her proficiency in playing parts in several European languages, she didn't speak English well, and no one cared to risk a production starring a barely understandable Polish actress. It became obvious that she had to improve her ability with English, so she hired a tutor who was German. Helena's pronunciation inevitably carried a heavy accent.

None of the San Francisco theatrical producers were impressed with a Polish "countess" they considered merely a dilettante stepping out of the society world for a brief fling with acting, especially one with an accent. Then she was introduced to Miss Josephine Tuholski, a Polish woman who spoke excellent English. "Miss Jo" tutored Helena, and their work together led to a lifelong companionship between them. A natural aptitude for languages made Helena a quick study, and, in August of that same year, she made her debut on the American stage in *Adrienne Lecouvreur.*

The critics were largely complimentary, although the *San Francisco Chronicle* had little regard for her acting talents: "Few ladies have appeared on the San Francisco stage who have owed so much to womanly grace and sympathy and so little to distinguished talent."

Within a few months, however, she was on tour. Most reviews were glowing, with the occasional reservation expressed about a foreign actress. After two curtain calls at the opening of *Adrienne Lecouvreur* in Virginia City, Nevada, the *Territorial Enterprise* printed a glowing review. Another publication, however, called her acting "peculiar" and opted to observe other performances before casting a final opinion. According to the *Footlight*: "A critic can only judge properly by comparison, and the fact that the play she appeared in was an entirely strange one prevents any extended criticism. The audience especially, are powerless to judge her ability, unless she appears in some play in which our own great stars have appeared."

It took only one more performance to convince the *Footlight* critic, who then conceded that Helena Modjeska was a sterling artist and "indescribably womanly."

The *Reno Gazette* of October 29, 1877, quoted an unnamed "eastern dramatic writer" in the advance notice of a performance at Smith's Academy of Music in Reno:

> *Her enunciation is clear and distinct, and is not impaired by naturally peculiar accentuation, and her distribution of emphasis is perfect. She has a very melodious voice with a variety of pleasing modulations. She has proved herself to be an actress of great energy, capable of fine intuitions, and long experience on the Polish stage has made her a finished artist. Her figure is lithe, supple and graceful. She has a good and very refined face, and her power of expression is remarkable.*

Within six months the Polish colony near Anaheim had fragmented, but Helena's career had turned to solid gold. She went on to great acclaim in New York, where her husband joined her after finally disposing of their property. Playing Marguerite Gauthier in the play *Camille* the way she believed the author intended, she achieved huge success, with the theater sold out weeks in advance.

The script was not universally loved by actresses who played the part, nor by audiences who were somewhat scandalized by a play about a "fallen woman." Helena wrote: "It pleased my imagination to present [Marguerite Gauthier] in *Camille* as reserved, gentle, intense in her love, and most sensitive—in one word, an exception to her kind." Her insightful performances in various roles were the result of study and a desire to strictly follow the intentions of the author of the play.

She did not like what had happened in American theater where a "star" system had taken hold. Theater managers knew a leading actor could fill the house and exploited that fact wherever they could. Helena thought American actors never developed a good range because they followed too closely what managers dictated rather than demand new, challenging parts in order to develop their repertoire in depth.

Otis Skinner, an actor who had worked with Helena at the Baldwin Theater in San Francisco, compared her with the leading actresses of the day who played the same parts. *Camille* was a play that had been adapted from a French novel by Alexandre Dumas, son of the man of the same name famous for *The Three Musketeers*. The French title, translated *The Lady of the Camellias*, had been shortened to *Camille* in America. It tells the story of a courtesan, Marguerite, who falls in love with a gentle young man; to be worthy of his love she tries to escape the life she has been leading. The youth's father persuades her to give him up so as not to ruin the boy's future and that of his innocent adolescent sister. Heeding the father's plea, she breaks her young lover's heart and her own by returning to her life as a courtesan and dies alone and poor, only sending him her journal at her death with the truth behind her betrayal of their love.

Modjeska dug deep to find the heart of her character, and Skinner recognized her genius:

> *Where Mme. Modjeska's art was greater than that of any other actress was in its womanliness, its joyousness and its limpid purity. She played Camille, even, with such serene sweetness that the unworthy in the character was forgotten and only the intrinsic womanliness of the role was presented. Mme. Sarah Bernhardt's Camille was a technical triumph. It was finished with a diamond cutter's skill, but it was theatrical, objective and studied. [Eleanora] Duse's Camille was a magnificent performance of hard, unlovely realism, which grew in effect as it grew in unpleasantness. It was big and brutal. Mme. Modjeska's Camille was the work of a poetess, whose soul, sensitive to suffering, comprehended Camille's misery and reflected it, as a pool of water reflects an object—without contamination, or offense.*

Following that success, Helena's family joined her to visit Europe, but she returned several times to America where she traveled on tour in a stylish and comfortable private railroad car. She and her husband had become naturalized citizens and, when not on tour, lived again in Southern California. Ironically they had come almost full circle, for the estate they purchased in Santiago Canyon was only about twenty miles from the ill-fated utopian colony that had inspired their journey from Poland to America.

She named the new estate Arden. A large addition to the original ranch house was designed by famed architect Stanford White and included a front entrance resembling a stage, where impromptu performances took place. Helena designed gardens where she could walk in peace among her roses. She toured for twenty years, always returning to Arden to rest and recuperate from bouts of ill health. In 1888 and 1889 she played roles she had always loved (including Lady Macbeth, Ophelia, Beatrice, Viola, Portia, and Rosalind) while on tour with Edwin Booth, the great Shakespearean actor.

Her great skill in holding an audience came from her deep belief in playing a part in such a natural way that the audience tended to forget they were watching a drama. Each role was analyzed and rehearsed to spellbinding perfection. Once, she recalled after the birth of her son's first child, she had half jokingly promised that she would convincingly play Juliet when she had become a grandmother. She succeeded because her ability transcended the knowledge of the audience that she was not the teenager in love who Shakespeare had so accurately portrayed with his pen.

The *Territorial Enterprise* of Nevada recognized that ability during her first appearances in America in 1877. Following the performances in windswept Virginia City, the jokes about a Polish-born actress died away. Said the *Enterprise* critic: "The audience listened as to an incantation and went away believers in enchantment. We cannot, in a brief and hurried notice, give any idea of the acting of Madame Modjeska. She is a lady of wonderful mind, and that mind has been trained in the severe discipline of the European schools, until art has become so perfect that it seems like nature."

The freedoms of America were as important to Helena and her husband as the money earned on the stage. Still, despite her long and successful career in America, a large corner of her heart belonged to Poland. As it had been when she and her husband had been shadowed by secret police for their outspoken views on the heavy-handed Prussian regime, her voice was raised again at the World's Columbian Exposition at Chicago in 1893. She drew a large crowd impatient to see the woman who had reportedly mesmerized an audience simply by reciting the Polish alphabet. Her unusual speech galvanized the audience even though it delved into international affairs and foreign policy. She censured those who oppressed her native land and its women.

In 1907 she and her husband left their Santiago Canyon retreat and moved to a small home on Bay Island, near Newport Beach. Although her health had improved during the years in America, she was ill much of the time and saw few visitors. Helena Modjeska died on April 8, 1909. Her remains were returned to Poland where they were interred in Cracow, the city of her birth.

# Matilda Heron

## The Star of the American Theatre

*Never have we seen a popular enthusiasm more fervid and un-remitting than what Miss Heron has created. Night after night her houses have not only been filled, but crowded and the ardent thousands who have contributed to her applause seem to have been governed by a feeling of direct and active personal interest in her welfare.*

—*California Chronicle*, San Francisco,
January 30, 1854

The American Theatre in San Francisco stood patiently waiting for patrons to fill its empty hall. The building was a simple structure with a moderate-size stage and kerosene footlights. It had played host to many of the aspiring entertainers of the early Gold Rush days. At one time its seats had been filled to capacity every night, but now times had changed. The new Metropolitan Theater, billed as "the most gorgeous theater in the United States," was attracting the clientele that had previously flocked to the American. It would take an incredible talent to save the play-house now. It was late December 1853, and the managers of the American were making plans to close down the hall.

Actor James Murdock convinced them to keep the doors open for a performance from a thespian he had worked with in Boston—a show for whomever would attend.

On Monday, December 26, Matilda Heron, a very young and not yet celebrated actress, stepped out onto the American

Theatre stage and instantly captured the hearts of the audience seated before her. She portrayed the character Bianca from the play *Fazio* and transported the crowd to another place and time with her talent.

By the end of the week, she was playing to a full house every night, resuscitating the expiring American and halting the theater's early demise. Critics proclaimed that her success lay in "her perfect naturalness of manner, the total absence of those screamings, rantings, and gesticulations which have grown up rank and deep-rooted weeds on the dramatic field!" Four weeks after her arrival in the West, Matilda had become the star she'd always dreamed of being.

Matilda Agnes Heron was born on December 1, 1830, in Londonderry, Ireland. Her parents were John Heron and Mary Laughlin Heron, and she was the youngest of five children, all of whom were educated in private schools. Shortly after she turned twelve, her father moved the family to Philadelphia, Pennsylvania, where he prospered as a merchant. His income allowed him to send Matilda to a French academy. There, influenced by one of her teachers, she developed an interest in the theater.

Matilda's first efforts in the arts were in the fields of poetry and literature. She was successful to a fair extent, but the praise she received was not prompt or palpable enough for her practical and ardent mind. She felt the stage was a more fitting challenge and decided to pursue acting as her profession, against the wishes of her fiercely religious parents, who believed actors were in a league with the devil himself. For three years she studied under master thespian Peter Richings in "the private philosophy of the stage."

As soon as she had completed her studies, she stepped onto the stage of the Walnut Street Theatre in Philadelphia. It was 1851, and every noteworthy actor and actress of the time had played the Walnut. Dignitaries, including presidents, attended shows there. Audiences were awed by her performance in the play *Camille*. She possessed a grace and ease that many of her fellow thespians admired. According to reviews of the time, her performances were "loaded with emotional intensity."

Talent agent George Lewis was quick to recognize her potential and convinced her to let him be her representative. George believed she could earn a great deal of money performing for entertainment-starved miners in California. Two years after her debut in Philadelphia, she and George were on their way to San Francisco by steamer.

The ocean voyage west, however, was a tragic one. George became ill along the way and died six days before their inbound steamer docked on December 25, 1853. Matilda was alone, and her arrival went unnoticed. Just before she was scheduled to board another steamer to take her back east, she met James Murdock, a noted tragedian with whom she had worked in the past. If not for him, her career in California would never have started. Learning of her plight and attesting to her talents, Murdock convinced the owners of the American Theatre to let Matilda perform there.

Frank Soule of the *California Chronicle* marveled at the audience's response to her performance on opening night:

> *Nevertheless, on the night of the 26th of December, the American Theatre was thrilled to host the friendless candidate's performance. A burst of welcome greeted her entrance, and then the house subsided into a state of nervous anxiety, such as, perhaps, was never felt before, for a person so entirely unknown. She spoke; a profound silence followed, which showed that every mind was working on her merits; she spoke again, and a breath of satisfaction and relief could be audibly distinguished. At length the process of the piece brought her to one of those points which enable her to show, in pathos, the deep harmonious music of the soul, and then burst forth a cheer that made the building shake. Suspense was over; she was received into the innermost appreciation of her audience, and all concern for her future success, by those who had assumed the responsibility of an opinion in advance, was lost in an enthusiasm that knew no bounds. Her triumph was not confined to*

The Metropolitan Theatre was one of the most respected theatres in the Old West COURTESY OF THE CALIFORNIA HISTORY ROOM, CALIFORNIA STATE LIBRARY, SACRAMENTO, CALIFORNIA

*the front; even the actresses embraced and kissed her, and she was equally petted before and behind the curtain.*

Summing up her successful engagement, Soule wrote, "She has played twelve nights in the test characters of the tragic drama, and after a success unparalleled, closed with a reputation which places her at the very pinnacle of fame. . . . Genius alone can excite such a sentiment as this, and they who win it have reason to thank Heaven, for they are the favored of the gods."

Historian John H. McCabe wrote often of Matilda's extraordinary talent and generosity. His unpublished theatrical journal notes that on December 30, 1854, Matilda donated the proceeds from her performance to her agent's widow. She insisted that the money be sent back to Mrs. Lewis by the next eastbound steamer.

McCabe wrote that many were impressed by Matilda's gift and were anxious to reward her for showing such kindness: "This noble conduct, struck from the soul under circumstances which forbids all suspicion of artifice, became known through members of the company, and before night a number of gentlemen spontaneously contributed to the purchase of a diamond cross for the generous girl, as an appropriate reward of an act of such pious and munificent charity."

Reporter Frank Soule, on hand the evening the diamond cross was presented to the adored actress, was equally moved,

> We do not recollect ever to have beheld a scene of equal excitement in a theater to the one exhibited during the presentation of that jewel.
>
> Ignorant of what was to be said or done (for the whole arrangement was but a few hours old), Miss Heron was called before the curtain with the theater manager. The whole house rose, and her arrival at the center of the stage was the signal for a shower of bouquets, too numerous to be gathered, which literally deluged her feet. "What will she do with them all?" said a voice during a momentary lull. "She'll walk upon them!" was the answer of a dozen, and three cheers endorsed the sentiment.
>
> At this moment a large and magnificent bunch of flowers was handed by a gentleman from the crowded corner of the orchestra, on the top of which glittered the sparkling present, and beside it a note which the theater manager was requested to read. "Dear Young Lady—A few among the thousands whom your merits have already made your friends in California desire to present you this small evidence of their esteem. It is a symbol of the religion you profess, and we trust that while it reminds you of your faith, it will at the same time be received as a pledge that genius never can be friendless on these shores.

Many emotions crossed Matilda's face as she listened to the words. She laughed, cried, and then made a short speech thanking the gentlemen for their kindness, after which she "was lodged

Matilda Heron

firmly in the hearts of that transported audience . . . so that 'six yoke of oxen could not drag her out,'" according to the *Chronicle*.

The proceeds from the evening's benefit came to more than sixteen hundred dollars. At the end of Matilda's first week at the American, management presented her with an extra five hundred dollars as an acknowledgment of her role in keeping the theater open against the formidable attractions of the competing Metropolitan.

Matilda's run at the American Theatre included stellar performances in such shows as *The Countess of Love*, *The Wife*, *Love's Sacrifice*, *The Honeymoon*, and *The Stranger*. One local reviewer confessed that he had been so moved by Miss Heron's representation of Mrs. Haller in *The Stranger* that "he would never dare to undergo the ordeal of seeing a repetition of that performance."

A reporter for the *San Francisco Evening Bulletin* had lavish praise for her performance as Juliana in *The Honeymoon*:

> *Throughout the changes of that metamorphosis she was true to nature and to reason. The natural vanities of the giddy girl, her ambition of the coronet, her indignation when convinced of the deception practiced upon her, her resistance to the authority of her husband, her deception to regain her freedom and divorce, the gradual change wrought by love and association, and the full gush of love at last, with the delight of gratified pride which comes as a crown to love, and her own reformation in temper and manner, were all given with a truthfulness to nature that carried everything before it, no less the hearts than the heads of the audience.*

Matilda Heron finished her opening season in Gold Rush Country to great fanfare. Frank Soule summed up her California triumph:

> *A debut among strangers, without prestige—twelve remarkable performances—two occasions when the sale of tickets was stopped in the afternoon—and a benefit at the*

*conclusion, when, despite storms, the counter attractions
of a grand oratorio at Musical Hall, and an imposing
military display at the Metropolitan, she, on the short notice of a day, drew a densely crowded house. She has therefore won every description of endorsement, as well from
actors as from the public and the press, and she stands a
fixed dramatic identity; a dazzling star, whose radiance
will always shine preeminent, by whatever constellation it
may be surrounded.*

During her stay in San Francisco, Matilda met Henry H.
Byrne, a handsome prominent attorney with the Mission Dolores
law firm. In June 1854, the two were secretly married in a private ceremony, and, according to the custom of the day, Matilda
retired from the theater. She longed for the footlights, however,
and returned to acting three weeks later, an action that so horrified
her new husband that they separated.

Humiliated and heartbroken, Matilda left California and
headed back to Philadelphia. She joined a prestigious acting troupe
and traveled to Washington, Chicago, and New York. Along the
way she perfected her portrayal of Camille in the play of the same
name, prompting theater critics across the country to proclaim her
"the most sensational Camille in America."

In December 1857 Matilda entered into a second marriage,
this time with conductor and composer Robert Stoepel. The two
had a daughter they named Helene. The marriage was not a happy
one, and Matilda sought refuge in her work, traveling again with
the Philadelphia based acting troupe, with her daughter by her
side. She returned to California in 1865. This time the rave reviews
were not only for her performances but for her daughter's as well.
Seven-year-old Helene performed under the stage name Bijou
Heron and was called a brilliant singer and actress.

Matilda and Robert Stoepel divorced in 1869. She lost herself in her work again, taking time to write, produce, and star in
her own plays. She created a sensation wherever she performed.

Her acting style was unique, as she followed her feelings rather than the rules of elocution, eschewing the use of grand gestures and booming variations of the voice. She hypnotized audiences and critics alike with her dark, flashing eyes, which transformed her otherwise plain face.

By the early 1870s her health was failing. Her once slender figure grew corpulent, and her rich, dark hair turned gray. Her popularity began to wane. She had to supplement her dwindling income by teaching drama and stage performance.

Her last years were not happy ones. She acted some but was ill and impoverished. Over the course of her career, she had earned more than two hundred thousand dollars playing Camille alone. Now, at the age of forty-two, she was broke, having lost all her money to extravagant living and lavish generosity. On January 17, 1872, a benefit was held for her in New York. A total of four thousand dollars was raised to help sustain the actress.

Matilda ended her acting career on the same stage on which she'd begun it—the Walnut Street Theatre in Philadelphia. During the 1874–1875 season she portrayed an array of emotional characters, including Lady Macbeth. Her daughter, who by this time had established herself as a successful actress, was a constant source of happiness to her in her final years. (Helene later went on to marry the celebrated actor Henry Miller and became the mother of theatrical producer Gilbert Heron Miller.)

Early in 1877 Matilda's ill health necessitated an operation, from which she did not recover. She subsequently died at the age of forty-seven at her New York City home. Matilda was laid to rest in Greenwood Cemetery in Brooklyn.

# Mary Anderson

## The Self-Made Star

*I intend to play westward, and to appear in the town in which I was born—Sacramento.*

—MARY ANDERSON'S COMMENTS TO A REPORTER AT THE *SAN FRANCISCO CALL*, 1886

The angry hawk clenched its talons on the heavy leather gauntlet, stabbing the delicate wrist beneath. Wings bated, the half-wild bird glared fiercely into the large gray eyes of his captor. Mary Anderson stared back with steely determination. This unruly bird would be tamed, she resolved, and would become a living prop for her performance of the Countess in Sheridan Knowles's comedy, *Love*. A stuffed bird would not provide the realism she intended, and what Mary Anderson intended usually came to be. Mary wrote in her memoirs:

> *There is a fine hawking scene in one of the acts, which would have been spoiled by a stuffed falcon, however beautifully hooded and gyved he might have been; for to speak such words as: How nature fashion'd him for his bold trade, /Gave him his stars of eyes to range abroad, / His wings of glorious spread to mow the air, /And breast of might to use them to an inanimate bird, would have been absurd.*

Always absolutely serious about her profession, Mary procured a half-wild bird and set to work on bending its spirit to her will.

127

The training, she explained, started with taking the hawk from a cage and feeding it raw meat "hoping thus to gain his affections." She wore heavy gloves and goggles to protect her eyes. The hawk was not easily convinced of her motives, and "painful scratches and tears were the only result."

She was advised to keep the bird from sleeping until its spirit broke, but she refused to take that course. Persevering with the original plan, Mary continued to feed and handle the hawk until it eventually learned to sit on her shoulder while she recited her lines, then fly to her wrist as she continued; then, at the signal from her hand, the bird would flap away as she concluded with a line about a glorious, dauntless bird. The dauntless hawk and Mary Anderson were birds of a feather.

Born July 28, 1859, at a hotel in Sacramento, California, Mary's earliest years were unsettled. Her mother, Antonia Leugers, had eloped with Charles Henry Anderson, a young Englishman intent on finding his fortune in America. It was a love match not approved by Antonia's parents. The young couple arrived in Sacramento in time for Mary's birth but too late to scoop up a fortune from the nearest stream. The easy pickings of the 1849 Gold Rush were gone.

Disappointed, the family returned east to Louisville, Kentucky, where Mary's uncle was the priest in a small settlement near the city. Her father joined the Confederate Army and died in battle when she was three. A few years later her mother married Dr. Hamilton Griffin. Despite the strong guidance Griffin provided for his stepchildren, Mary, at least, went her headstrong way almost from the first.

"It was my desire to be always good and obedient, but, like 'Cousin Phoenix's legs,' my excellent intentions generally carried me in the opposite direction," Mary wrote in her memoirs. "On seeing a minstrel show for the first time I was fired with a desire to reproduce it. After a week of plotting with [my brother] Joe

I invited Dr. Griffin and my mother to the performance of the nature of which they were utterly ignorant."

The performance took place in the family's front parlor, which was divided by double doors. The audience sat in back, and when the folding doors were thrown open, Mary's stunned parents took in the scene. "My baby sister and I were discovered as 'end men.' She was but eight months old and tied to a chair. Our two small brothers sat between us, and we were all as black as burnt cork rubbed in by my managerial hands could make us." To top off the visual shock, Mary gaily began the opening chorus of the show: "Goodbye John! Don't stay long! Come back soon to your own chick-a-biddy."

That creative spirit and the will to back it up challenged the nuns at the Ursuline Convent Mary attended. They could not interest her in geography and arithmetic. "She was one of those children whose wild artistic nature chafes under the restraints of home and school life," wrote J. M. Farrar of her early years. "Indeed, her wildness acquired for her the name of 'Little Mustang.' The beautiful, headstrong little girl became a beautiful, headstrong woman who trained herself to become an actress who eventually became known in the western states as 'Our Mary.'"

Mary was twelve years old and already memorizing Shakespeare when she saw the famous Shakespearean actor Edwin Booth in *Hamlet*. At that point The Bard became her self-selected schoolmaster, and becoming an actress became her one burning goal. At thirteen she dropped out of school and began studying elocution with a nearby teacher, but, above all, she memorized lines and practiced roles on her own.

Mary was about fifteen when she got hold of copies of old playbooks, which she used to teach herself. A local theater character, Uncle Henry Davis, an aged prompter from the days when performances included an offstage voice, or prompter, reading lines the actors repeated, provided her with an invaluable aid. Davis took apart the playbooks, added blank pages, and then diagrammed stage positions and described on them the "stage business" necessary to a performance. As she paced about, thinking, memorizing, trying to understand the motivations of Shakespeare's heroines, Mary unconsciously worried the yellow-backed books with her teeth.

Two years later, almost completely self-taught, Mary made her debut at a Louisville theater. On Saturday, November 27, 1875, after only a single rehearsal, she played Juliet before a packed house. The next morning the *Louisville Courier* praised her performance as a great actress but did not overlook her faults:

> *In the latter scenes she interpreted the very spirit and soul of tragedy, and thrilled the whole house into silence by the depth of her passion and her power. . . . We owe it to her, for it is the greatest kindness, and yet we do not speak harshly and are glad to admit that most of her faults—such for instance as frequently casting up the eyes—are not only slight in themselves, but enhanced if not caused by the timidity natural on such an occasion.*

In February Mary again took the stage in Louisville, then opened in St. Louis and was invited to New Orleans, where, at the opening-night performance of *Evadne*, only forty-eight dollars was made in ticket sales. Nevertheless, young men in the audience from the military college nearby were so impressed by her beauty and passion that between acts they went out and bought up all the bouquets they could find—and the last act was played knee-deep in flowers. By the time she left New Orleans, the seventeen-year-old beauty was a star, and two Confederate generals and an admiring crowd saw her off at the train station.

Some criticism of her presentation appeared in newspapers and theater journals, but Mary was a sensation with the general public. It was early in 1876 when she, not yet eighteen, decided to tour the West. Accompanied by her mother and stepfather, Dr.

Mary Anderson in *Winter's Tales*
COURTESY OF THE LIBRARY OF CONGRESS

Griffin, who was now managing her career, Mary declared her intention to bypass San Francisco for her first performance. Instead she insisted on stopping first in the town of her birth, Sacramento. The people in the new state capital turned out to welcome her "home," but by the time she opened in San Francisco, she had acquired a few critics, some of whom considered her an empty-headed debutante like those in the city who wanted to become actresses. "We have some dozen or two in this little city alone," wrote an editor in the *San Francisco Call*, "and the dramatic fever is becoming as universal and epidemic as the epizooty among horses a season or two ago."

Mary was hardly prepared for the reception she received from the press or the other actors in the troupe:

> *My appearance in San Francisco at Mr. John Mc-Cullough's theatre soon followed, and was the most un-happy of my professional life. With but few exceptions, the members of the numerous company ridiculed my work. My poor wardrobe was a subject of special sport to the gorgeously dressed women; and unkind remarks about "the interloper" were heard on every side. The Press cut me up, or rather tried to cut me down, advising me to leave the stage. Continual taunts from actors and journalists nearly broke my spirit.*

Mary was concerned for McCullough's ticket sales as well as the assault on her pride as an actress. On the last few nights she played Meg Merrilees in *Guy Mannering*, her ghostly make-up was so successful her own mother didn't recognize her. That role and one other dramatic part gained "genuine enthusiasm," the newspapers reported by the end of her San Francisco engagement.

Like the hawk she'd trained, her spirit had received a shock, but her will remained unbroken. In the midst of the terrible reviews in the press, her hero, Edwin Booth, appeared. "He laughed at my idea of quitting the stage on account of the unkindness of my fellow actors," she recalled. "'I also am a fellow actor,' said he; 'I have sat through two of your performances from beginning to end—the first time I have done such a thing in years—and I have not only been interested, but impressed and delighted.'"

The remainder of the tour, which included an introduction to President Ulysses Grant, was highly successful. At her New York debut on November 12, 1877, she was considered to have "much dramatic potentiality." Her beauty was part of the attraction: "Tall, willowy, and young," the *Herald* described, with a "fresh, fair face" and a small, finely chiseled mouth, large almond-shaped eyes, and hair of light brown. She was beautiful, acknowledged the critics, but many found her lacking in feeling. One defender, however, spoke up on her behalf. Charles Wingate, author and historian, countered the prevailing opinion of Mary Anderson as cold or reserved:

> *From the time of her first appearance on November 27, 1875, at McCauley's Theatre in Louisville, Ky., when the California-born girl was in her seventeenth year, her Juliet, her Rosalind, her Parthenia, her Galatea, her Pauline, her Julia, had shown what popular favor a magnificent figure, a superb voice, and a natural tragic power could gain, even if command of pathos and naturalness in comedy acting were less marked; but at the same time, the world constantly repeated the two words 'cold' and 'stately.' Perdita, however, her last character on the stage, was a revelation.*

Wingate described how Mary played two parts, one serious and rather austere, the other a light-footed "gazelle" who sang and danced with the abandon of a gypsy, something she had never successfully accomplished in the past.

By 1883 she was headed for Shakespeare's home ground in England, and she made it a point to put on performances in Stratford-on-Avon. She drew huge crowds and achieved unprecedented popular acclaim. Still, many of the British critics were not pleased by the American import.

She appeared as Galatea, a part that begins with the actress draped in white, gracefully posed, impersonating a beautiful marble statue that is brought to life by the love of the sculptor, Pygmalion. The critics said the part was easy because she played many of her parts with all the emotion of a statue. "Even in her ingenious scenes of comedy," reported the *Morning Post*, "there is no more dramatic vivacity than might be looked for in a block of stone."

Other newspapers realized how popular she had become. Despite the critics, Mary caught and held her audiences. "So strong was the appeal of her acting that on one occasion, where, as Galatea, she turned toward the auditorium with arms outstretched crying 'The Gods will help me,' the whole gallery rose and roared back 'We will! We will!'"

In 1886 she returned in triumph to America. Marcus R. Mayer, an advance agent drumming up publicity for her tour, told a reporter for the *San Francisco Call* that Mary was earning unprecedented sums. "Miss Anderson's gains have been simply immense," reported Mayer to the newspaperman. "She drew $249,000 during her seven months in London. . . . Her receipts were larger than those of the famous Henry Irving and Ellen Terry, though she played in Mr. Irving's own theater." In New York she reportedly made $65,000, and three weeks in Boston netted $42,000. The entire tour in the East totaled $237,000, a huge sum of money in 1886.

The *Sacramento Union* published her itinerary: Denver, Salt Lake City, Sacramento, and then San Francisco. The second time around, San Francisco loved her. On April 4 the *San Francisco Call* detailed her training and its success: "The late Noble Butler grounded her in the use of the English language, and directed her literary work, besides developing her voice, the richness of which is one of her great charms. Mr. Wastell, the dancing master, taught her to dance and instructed her in posturing."

Mary described what she did to succeed at her chosen profession. She studied her characters and every word they uttered on stage and looked at the interaction between characters to pin down the psychology of her part. Physically, she worked hard at every move she performed. "Always on the alert for improvement," she said, she decided to try the Delsarte system of movement, an acting style in which the expression of inner emotion was released using voice and gestures. "I determined to study it. As far as mechanical exercises were concerned, it seemed perfect to me, for it overlooks no muscle or tendon of the face or body, and gives strength, suppleness and control over them all. The rest of the system I afterwards found it best to discard."

One of the weak points of the system's theory, Mary decided, was the belief that outward expression and movement awaken and control emotions, which she concluded was exactly the opposite of what actually happened.

> The development of these various types, with their natural personality, mannerisms, etc., is a most engrossing study. How would a man or woman weep under given circumstances? Would he or she weep at all? And so in joy as well as sorrow, under the influence of every emotion, they have their individual way of doing everything. The art is to make the character harmonious from beginning to end; and the greatest actor is he who loses his own personality in that of his role.

Since her days with the hawk, she had insisted on what was natural rather than melodramatic. Achieving that goal required deep analysis of reality and of the psychology of expression and emotion, with the aim of always portraying as true a character as possible.

Back in London in 1887, Mary presented a unique version of *The Winter's Tale*. It ran for 164 performances, and she played two parts, Hermione and Perdita, in each performance, something no other actress had attempted. In 1888 she brought the production back to America, but it ended abruptly in 1889. Some say Mary suffered a nervous breakdown. She herself put it differently:

> *At Washington [It was Inauguration Week, and Mr. Harrison had just been proclaimed President] I went through the first two nights. On Ash Wednesday the doctor thought me too tired to make the effort, and I did not appear. On Thursday, against his wishes and those of that kindest of impresarios, Henry E. Abbey, I insisted on acting. The first scenes of The Winter's Tale went very smoothly. The theatre was crowded. Perdita [one of the parts she played] danced apparently as gaily as ever, but after the exertion, fell fainting from exhaustion, and was carried off the stage.*

Mary explained that overwork caused the onstage blackout.

In *Shakespeare's Heroines of the Stage*, written in 1895, Charles Wingate wondered what might have happened had Mary not collapsed: "Curious it is to recall that one feature in this last stage character of Mary Anderson displayed for the first time an utter abandonment of the charge which, from the very first of her career, had been held up against her acting. All critics had admitted her natural beauty, all had commended her intelligence, and many had praised her for earnestness and strength. But all declared that she was cold and passionless."

Wingate found that Mary's final character had broken the mold: The quick-footed gazelle could scarcely have been more light of foot, more animated, or more fascinating in action. The wild gypsy-like dance showed a living picture of free, easy, voluptuous movement, so devoid of artificiality or restraint as to be as captivating as it was real for such an ideal country-bred character.

Who could have believed the stately Mary Anderson capable of such graceful romping?

At twenty-four years old, Mary retired from the stage. In her memoirs she commented on the decision: "After so much kindness from the public it seems ungrateful to confess that the practice of my art (not the study of it) had grown as time went on more and more distasteful to me."

Mary realized that being an actress was more than just immersing herself in her art—she recognized how the public came to feel an ownership interest in the life of an actor.

In speaking the words of Shakespeare, the poet who had awakened her to the dream of acting, had become a dull routine. She had been enamored with the characters wrought by Shakespeare's pen and as a girl had never contemplated what success in portraying those characters might cost: "To be conscious that one's person was a target for any who paid to make it one; to live for months at a time in a groove, with uncongenial surroundings, and in an atmosphere seldom penetrated by the sun and air; and to be continually repeated the same passions and thoughts and the same words—that was the most part of my daily life, and became so like slavery."

With characteristic determination, Mary Anderson retired at the peak of her popularity, just as she seemed to have overcome the one criticism that had dogged her career from the beginning. She had determined her course at the age of twelve, had worked to step onstage in a lead role, and did it at barely seventeen; she'd traveled across the United States on tour several times, made a tremendous amount of money before she was twenty, had convinced the British Isles that an American could play Shakespeare, and had broken tradition by being the first actress to play two parts in *The Winter's Tale*.

In effect, Mary Anderson had no life but her life on the stage. She may have feared the same fate as the young hawk she'd once trained. "As an actor," she said of the hawk, "his career was highly successful. But constant travel and change of climate proved too much for him. In spite of the greatest care, he at last succumbed, and our noble bird was buried in the alley back of McVicker's Theater, Chicago."

In June 1890 she married Antonio Fernando de Navarro, a wealthy American of Basque heritage who was said to have a claim on the throne of Spain. Mary met Tony when he arrived backstage after a performance. She'd refused his first requests to call on her, but she finally gave in and was impressed by the young man who looked and acted like a Spanish aristocrat. In her memoirs she recalled Tony telling her he vowed at that first meeting to marry her or become a priest.

The couple moved to Worcestershire, England. It was, according to her memoirs, a happy marriage that set her free from what she called bondage to the theater. She reveled in living naturally under the sun and the stars, rather than working to appear natural in a part written for a scene in a play performed under an artificial moon and fake stars suspended above the stage.

Mary and Tony were part of a wealthy, literate set that included famous writers, musicians, and playwrights. Their home was a mecca for artists, and Mary enjoyed riding and outdoor entertainments as well as domestic pursuits. Her first son died in infancy, but two other children prospered. Mary was continually asked to return to the stage, but her appearances were generally limited to charity work. During World War I she appeared on behalf of war charities and made visits to injured soldiers and women working in factories to support the war effort.

Tony died in 1932, and Mary lived another eight years, the last several of which she was seriously ill. Mary died in 1940 at the age of eighty at her home in England.

# Laura Keene

## The President's Actress

*The world called Laura Keene an actress. We call her a heroine.*

—Madison Wisconsin State Journal,
April 17, 1933

Mary Todd Lincoln screamed. Clara Harris, seated in the balcony adjacent to President Abraham Lincoln's wife, jumped out of her seat and rushed to the hysterical woman's side. "He needs water!" Harris cried out to the audience at Ford's Theatre staring up at her in stunned silence. "The President's been murdered!" The full ghastly truth of the announcement washed over the congregation, and the scene that ensued was as tumultuous and as terrible as one of Dante's pictures of hell. Some women fainted, others uttered piercing shrieks and cries for vengeance, and unmeaning shouts for help burst from the mouth of men. Beautiful, dark-haired actress Laura Keene hurried out from the wings dressed in a striking, maroon-colored gown under which was a hoop skirt and a number of petticoats that made the garment sway as she raced to a spot center stage. She paused for a moment before the footlights to entreat the audience to be calm. "For God's sake, have presence of mind, and keep your places, and all will be well." Laura's voice was a brief voice of reason in a chaotic scene. Few could bring their panic under control. Mary Lincoln was in shock and sat on her knees rocking back and forth beside her mortally wounded husband. She cradled her arms in her hands and sobbed uncontrollably.

Laura ordered the gas lights around the theater turned up. Patrons bolted toward the building's exits. As they poured out into the streets, they told passersby what had occurred. Crowds began to gather, and there were just as many people coming back into the theater as were trying to leave. Laura stepped down off the stage and began fighting against the current of people pressing all around her. Word began to pass through the frantic group that John Wilkes Booth was responsible for shooting the president. Sharp words were exchanged between the individuals coming in and going out of the building. Insane grief began to course through the theater, and ugly suppositions started to form. "An actor did this!" Laura wrote in her memoirs about what people were saying at the event. "The management must have been in on the plot! Burn the damn theatre! Burn it now!" Laura disregarded the remarks and somehow worked her way to the rear box where Mr. Lincoln was and stepped inside.

According to the biography of Laura Keene by Vernanne Bryan, when the actress entered the president's box he was lying on the floor. "At first glance it was as if he had only fallen and his usual black, unruly hair had simply become more tousled from the fall," Bryan reported what Laura witnessed. "But upon closer scrutiny, the picture became distorted and took on the shadowy quality of the non-rational, for under his great head, seeping slowly across the floor in a crimson pool, came his life's blood." Doctor Charles Leale was attending to President Lincoln while Laura was there and told other physicians on the scene that Mr. Lincoln's wounds were fatal. "It is impossible for him to recover," he is noted telling his colleagues.

Laura turned to Mrs. Lincoln who was crying and unable to speak and then asked the doctor if she could hold the president until he could be moved. Gently, Laura knelt down and lifted Mr. Lincoln's wounded head onto her lap. A bowl of water was brought to her, and she bathed his brow.

The locality of the wound was initially thought to have been in his chest. It was not until after the neck and shoulders had been bared and no mark discovered and Laura's dress was stained with blood that it was revealed where the ball had penetrated.

As soon as the confusion and the crowd were partially overcome, the president was moved to a home across the street from the theater. Laura remained on the floor for a moment, watching for members from Thompson's Battery C, Pennsylvania's Light Artillery, maneuver Mr. Lincoln's lanky frame into the home where he would later be pronounced dead. At the urging of army guards who were summoned to the scene, Laura picked herself up and escorted the shocked, wide-eyed Mary to the boarding house where her husband's body was located. Laura stayed with the president's wife until the carriage came to escort his body away.

Laura Keene was considered by many familiar with her work as an actress and theater manager to be the greatest woman ever connected with the American stage. In spite of her pioneering efforts in the field, she would be more closely identified with Ford's Theatre and Lincoln's assassination than anything she ever did in the profession.

The incomparable Laura Keene was born in Paris in 1826. Her parents, who named their daughter Mary Frances, were well-read and believed their children needed a well-rounded education. Laura and her brothers and sisters were exposed to art, literature, and music and were encouraged to try their hand at each. Laura, a dark-haired beauty with large honey-brown eyes had a talent for painting but was particularly intrigued with the theater. She couldn't resist stopping outside the window of the local playhouse and listening to the actors perform. From an early age she knew she was destined for the stage.

Laura's father died when she was fifteen, and the family struggled financially. She was determined to find work to help support her mother and siblings. Laura found employment as a bar-

Laura Keene

maid at a pub in London and served ice cream at a cafe in Surrey. While employed at the tavern, she met Henry Wellington Taylor, an officer in the British Army nine years her junior. He was very protective of Laura and promised if she married him to take care of her and her widowed mother. Laura agreed, and the pair wed on April 8, 1844. Henry purchased a pub on Oxford Street, and the couple lived above the establishment with her mother, Henry's aunt, and three household servants. Laura worked as a barmaid for the next seven years. The Taylors had two daughters. Emma was born in January 1845, and Clara was born in October 1848.

By 1851 Laura's marriage to Henry was ending. Henry had been involved in a number of criminal activities and arrested by British officials. He was deported and incarcerated in a penal colony somewhere in Australia. Laura attempted to file for divorce but could not locate Henry to begin the process. She eventually abandoned the pub and moved in with her aunt, an accomplished, retired actress with ties to the London theatrical scene.

Laura's aunt saw massive potential in her niece's natural talent for acting and helped her secure a job as a stock player at a theater. The entry level position gave Laura the opportunity to hone her skills portraying a variety of utilitarian parts, small roles as a townsperson, household staff member, innkeeper, and so on. She earned six dollars a week at the start. As Laura proved herself to be a steady and serviceable player, she was allowed to take on more difficult roles. Her salary increased to thirty dollars a week in a short nine months. On October 28, 1851, she made her London debut in *The Lady of Lyons* at the Olympic Theatre. Utilizing the techniques her aunt had taught her and under the tutelage of celebrated actor and manager Henry Farren, Laura entertained audiences with her poignant, moving portrayal of the play's heroine, Pauline Deschapelles.

Laura's performance was well received, and she followed the success with another stellar appearance in the popular play *As*

*You Like It.* According to the November 8, 1851, edition of the *London Lady's Newspaper* and pictorial, she was a "delight." The article explained,

> *Miss Laura Keene has appeared in the character of Rosalind in As You Like It, which is perhaps one of the most difficult parts to be found in Shakespeare's plays for it requires in it the combined excellence of the pathetic with the comic muse. Rosalind is too often mistaken for a mere frivolous, high-spirited girl; whilst, in truth, her liveliness is, as it were, a disguise under which a mind full of profound philosophy is ever at work. In the lively blaze of the character Miss Laura Keene shone conspicuously, but somewhat failed in displaying the deeper workings of a sensitive heart; but, taking Miss Keene's performance as a whole, it was highly creditable. She will prove a great acquisition to this pleasant little theatre.*

One year after her initial performance in London, Laura was enroute to the United States. She had aspirations of managing a theater of her own and was persuaded by her colleagues that in America she would have a chance to achieve her goal. Prior to setting sail for New York, Laura had secreted a position with respected actor James Wallack's stock company. He was there to meet her when she arrived in the country and presented her with the play in which she would be starring, entitled *The Will.* Laura made her New York debut on September 20, 1852, at Wallack's Theatre. Critics praised the sweet "English" sound of her speech and were enamored with her classic beauty and aristocratic manner. In a single evening, she had stolen the heart of New York.

James cast the popular actress in a series of other plays that drew more people to the theater. Soon the audience was demanding to see only Laura in lead roles and particularly in comedies. She had exceptional timing and excelled in comic performances. Although Laura was a major draw at Wallack's Theatre, her pay was less than half what lead actors received. The forty-five dollars she earned a week was not enough to support herself and her children in London, and she couldn't afford tickets for her daughters to come and live with her. Believing theatergoers would much more likely come to see the talented star if she was unencumbered with a spouse and children, James refused to increase Laura's salary.

The determined mother decided to pursue other avenues of earning a living and began contemplating a career as a theater manager. She signed on for a second season with James's company, but tucked in the back of her mind was the idea of leasing and managing her own group. She was contemplating the possibility of such a venture one night after the close of a show in January 1853. Laura was racing from the theater away from a number of well-dressed admirers vying for her attention when she nearly mowed over John Lutz. John was a gambler and well-connected American who would play an important part in her future endeavors.

Laura and John found in one another a fondness for the stage and an entrepreneurial spirit that made them believe anything was possible. Like Laura, John had a tumultuous marriage in his past, and he had a daughter. The pair quickly fell in love and forged a business partnership as well as a romantic one. When James denied Laura a raise for the second time, she asked John to investigate a theater for lease in Baltimore. His report back to her about the property was favorable. Laura asked James for a couple of days off from work to attend to personal business; she had decided to see the theater in Baltimore for herself. James refused to give her the time. Laura left for the weekend anyway.

According to the December 1, 1853, edition of the *Boston Post,* when the actress returned from Baltimore she found her name had been taken off the theater billing. Laura's relationship with the management at Wallack's Theatre continued to deteriorate, and, by mid-December 1853, she severed ties with the company.

On Christmas Eve 1853, Laura Keene assumed responsibility for operating the Charles Street Theatre in Baltimore, Maryland.

She opened with a play entitled *Hearts Are Trumps*. When the lights came up on the presentation, Laura became the first notable woman in America to manage a theater and production.

Laura focused on securing quality actors for her stock company. She selected people who were equally good at performing comedy and dramas. She secured skilled costume and wardrobe designers, artists who could create the backdrops and scenery, and detail-oriented builders who could construct sets. The result of her efforts was reflected in the reviews she received from a theater critic at the *Baltimore Sun* newspaper. According to the January 2, 1854, edition of the publication, the Charles Street Theatre was "the chief destination for playgoers." "The company performing at this elegant theatre is worthy to be styled a 'Star Company,'" the article read. "Miss Laura Keene, who is herself an actress of rare ability, has evinced great judgment in the selection of performers, and hence every play is placed upon the stage in the most effective manner. There is also great attention paid to the properties, the furniture, etc. being costly and beautiful."

Not only did Laura select the plays, cast, and crew, but she also performed in the productions as well. Her schedule was grueling. Between December 24, 1853, and February 23, 1854, she produced thirty-four different plays. Laura's health suffered under the pressure of managing so many projects, and, on February 25, 1854, she announced she would be leaving Baltimore and heading west.

Laura's stay at the Charles Street Theatre had been brief, less than three months. Although she cited exhaustion as a reason for departing Maryland, many fans believed she was attracted by the rumor of the large sums of money to be earned by performers in California.

The Gold Rush had let loose a floodgate of humanity onto the wild frontier. Hundreds of hopeful prospectors lined the creek beds and mountainsides from San Francisco to Sacramento.

Laura Keene's Theatre in Washington, D.C.
COURTESY OF THE LIBRARY OF CONGRESS

Entertainment was at a premium in the mining camps and gold towns; Laura planned to tap into the need for talent in the region and make a tidy profit doing so. On April 6, 1854, Laura debuted at the Metropolitan Theatre in San Francisco. Laura's mother and daughters were seated in the front row to watch the actress perform. John Lutz waited in the wings for his ingénue.

John had negotiated the contract Laura received from the management at the theater. She was to be paid thirty thousand dollars a year. Reviews in the leading Northern California newspapers about Laura's first performance in the play *The Love Chase* proved the investment made to retain the actress was money well spent. An article in the April 4, 1854, edition of the *Daily Alta California* noted,

*To those who have seen Laura Keene, she requires no fur-
ther recommendation as an actress than can be gathered
from noticing an evening's performance. She is a woman
on whose features genius is so indelibly stamped that it is
impossible not to admire her at first glance. As an actress
she possesses a happy power of combining a high degree of
art with naturalness, and her whole appearance and action upon the stage are irresistibly agreeable. She is an
actress of great versatility. She is an authoress as well as
an actress, and has written some sketches, marked with
decided ability and intellectual power.*

On stage Laura was poised and in control; behind the scenes,
however, she had difficulties with the brooding and temperamental
twenty-year-old actor named Edwin Booth playing opposite her.
Edwin was one of four children born into a theatrical family. His
father, Junius Brutus Booth, was a well-trained, gifted thespian.
Edwin was talented, but his moody personality and bouts of inse-
curity over his future on stage exasperated Laura.

John was aware of the strife brewing between Laura and
Edwin and sought to put an end to the situation before she was
taxed beyond her limits. John suggested a tour of the mining
towns that included engagements in Sacramento, Marysville,
and Stockton. Theatrical critics at the *Sacramento Daily Union*
newspaper called her acting "superior" and referred to her as
"accomplished and refined." Audiences in Stockton appreciated
the performer's appearance there, too. The April 26, 1854, edition
of the *San Joaquin Republican* reported that Laura "delighted the
public with her fresh and piquant style."

Laura's travels through the gold country ended back in
San Francisco, where she became sole manager and lessee of the
Union Theatre. The three-story building was located in the French
quarter of the city and was in need of refurbishing. Laura and
John immediately went to work redecorating and remodeling the
interior. Laura hired her favorite actors to be a part of the stock

company and scheduled rehearsals for two plays. The June 29, 1854, edition of the *Daily Alta California* announced the opening of the refitted theater and encouraged people to attend the show. "The house has been redone and is one of the neatest and prettiest theatrical establishments in the country," the article read. "Boucicault's new comedy *The School for Scheming* is cast with the entire strength of the excellent company. The performance will close with a new local burlesque entitled *The Camp* at the Union. We know that Miss Keene will use every exertion in her power to render the Union a pleasing place of resort and we do not doubt that our citizens will fully appreciate her labors."

The Union Theatre prospered under Laura's tutelage, and for a while her professional and personal life were thriving. In late July 1854, a fellow thespian returning to the United States from a tour in Australia informed Laura that she had heard that her estranged husband was in prison near Victoria. Laura told John the news and explained her need to acquire a divorce at long last. In order to expedite the dissolution of the marriage she had to travel to Australia to start the proceedings. John listened sympathetically and then shared information he'd been keeping to himself about his spouse. His estranged wife was suffering with terminal cancer and John felt, for the sake of his daughter in Georgetown, that his place was with her. Laura would have to go to Australia alone.

After making arrangements for her mother and children to return to New York, Laura boarded a ship bound for the Australian continent. Traveling with the determined actress was Edwin Booth. Gold had been discovered in the country in 1850, and by 1854 thousands had invaded it hoping to find the Mother Lode. Edwin heard performers could earn a small fortune as a part of reparatory theater companies in Australia. Upon hearing the news that Laura was going abroad, Edwin persuaded her to join him and another accomplished actor, Dave Anderson, in the venture. On July 31, 1854, Laura boarded the ship the *Mary Ann Jones* and set sail across the Pacific.

Laura and Edwin reconciled their differences enroute to Sydney. It took more than two months to reach Australia, and the actors became intertwined during the journey. For a brief moment in time, Edwin was not only Laura's lover but her confidant as well. In the years to come, she would regret any involvement she had had with him. Edwin was extremely competitive and used the ideas Laura had for producing particular plays as his own. In 1864, the pair were at odds over *Our American Cousin* and who had the rights to stage the show after the assassination of President Lincoln.

Laura, Edwin, and Dave Anderson opened in Sydney on October 23, 1854, in *The Lady of Lyons*. The three actors toured major cities throughout the country until early February 1855. Laura received outstanding reviews everywhere she performed, and often her name was listed first by the critics praising the show. Edwin was annoyed by the attention Laura was getting and made it known to his cast members that he was unhappy. Using his poor behavior as a reason to leave, Laura severed all ties with the company. She hired a small troupe of her own to travel about performing and hired a detective to help her find her estranged husband. The search proved to be pointless. Try as they did, they could not locate Henry Taylor.

Laura returned to San Francisco on March 21, 1855. Her first performance in California after her tour through Australia was on March 27, 1855, at the Sacramento Theatre. She played Lady Gay Spanker in the comedy *London Assurance*. The show ran for only five nights, and, once the final curtain came down, Laura hurried back to San Francisco to appear at the American Theatre in a series of fan-favorite plays. Her opening performance was to take place on April 8, 1855, but an unfortunate accident kept Laura from the stage. The April 9, 1855, edition of the *San Francisco*

*Daily Sun* reported the particulars of the situation. "While Miss Keene was passing along the sidewalk between her place of residence and the American Theatre she made a false step in which her right ancle [sic] was sprained," the article read. "Unfortunately this is the second occurrence of the kind to the same limb within the past year which renders the casualty more painful. Owing to this mishap the opening of the American Theatre was postponed until this evening."

A decidedly pleased audience cheered the actress's performances at the American Theatre. After only a couple of weeks, Laura was not only performing but also managing the playhouse. San Francisco patrons were demanding plays, and she was lavishly producing them. Whether Laura was publicizing a new show or performing as the lead in a dramatic or light comic opera, her work was appreciated. "Much as we are disposed to admire the excellence of this lady in more serious or heavier parts," an article in the May 5, 1855, edition of the *Daily Alta California* read, "we must own that in comic representation Miss Keene displays a freshness and peculiar relish for the part she is playing which irresistibly carries the audience with her and excites a ready response in the heart of listeners."

Laura was given the official title of directoress at the American Theatre in June 1855. Once again the *Daily Alta California* praised the lady theatrical pioneer's diversity remarking in its June 11, 1855, edition that Laura's "remarkable cleverness in adopting and bringing out pieces such as suit the popular taste."

In September 1855, residents in the city of San Francisco hailed Laura as "the actress of all work" and credited her with "revitalizing theatre in the Gold Country." The community at large was broken hearted when Laura made the announcement that she would be vacating her position at the American Theatre and returning to the East Coast. On October 4, 1855, the people of San Francisco demonstrated their affection for her by packing the house of the theater. According to the October 5, 1855, edition of the *Daily Alta California,*

> *It was one of the largest audiences ever crowded into the theatre, . . . . It is useless to attempt description of what transpired upon the stage. We walked from one of the three entrances to the parquetted, but such was the density of the crowds stationed at each that we could only now and then, by standing on tip-toe and elongating the neck to a painful degree, catch a glimpse of waving skirt and embroidered coat-tail or a powdered wig. Above the boxes the case was equally hopeless, but as we left the theatre in despair a tremendous round of applause gave token that it was all right within.*

News that Laura Keene was making her way to New York reached the papers in the city, and numerous fans eagerly looked forward to her arrival. Laura was excited about being reunited with her children and mother, but anxious over seeing John Lutz. There had been no communication between them since they separated in the summer of 1854. She hoped they would meet again, but didn't relish the thought of telling him she was still married. John was waiting for her at the docks when her ship arrived. He had read of her coming home in the *New York Daily Times.*

Laura and John's personal and professional relationship resumed. He understood that she was doing all she could to end her marriage and was eager to help her lease space at a theater of her own. The two worked in concert to achieve the goal, and, in late November 1855, they had purchased the Metropolitan Theatre on Broadway and were making the facility ready for the opening of the plays *Two Can Play at that Game* and *Prince Charming.*

Critics and audiences were pleased to see Laura on stage, but competing theater managers proved to be a challenge for her. James Wallack, her one time champion, spoke out against a woman being in a position of director and stage manager. Other men who operated theaters on Broadway echoed the sentiment. They resented her presence in the field, and, with every successful production Laura achieved, their hostility grew. Unknown individuals broke into her playhouse in late December 1855 and not only vandalized the building but also destroyed sets and scenery. The police conducted an investigation, but no arrests were made. With John's help Laura repaired the damage and pressed on.

In June 1856 William Burton, owner and manager of Burton's Theatre, and competitor of Laura Keene's establishment, purchased the building she was leasing. Burton evicted Laura, and subsequently her production came to an abrupt end. According to the June 18, 1856, edition of the *New York Herald*, "the managers at rival theatres were against Laura from the onset. Perhaps on the principle that so long kept votes from women."

Laura took her predicament to the public who adored her. She submitted letters to the *New York Daily Times* and the *New York Herald* explaining that she had invested all she had financially into the theater she had lost and had nothing left to start over. Hundreds of thousands of dollars were contributed by fans who wanted to help her build a place of her own.

Laura Keene's new theater seated twenty-five hundred and was praised by patrons as the most gorgeous hall in the city. For seven seasons, a time period from November 1856 to 1863, Laura presented shows that entertained and excited audiences. She made a serious effort to produce original plays. One of her favorites was penned by Tom Taylor, an English dramatist and magazine editor who wrote more than one hundred plays in his career. The play was entitled *Our American Cousin*. Laura believed so strongly in the potential of Taylor's three-act play that she ordered a copyright on the material and claimed ownership rights and even gave the play its name.

In January 1863 Laura hired a stock company to tour America. She accompanied them and starred in productions performed in Boston, Philadelphia, and Washington. *Our American Cousin* was the highlight of the repertoire. The play is the story of a gullible English baronet who entrusts his financial affairs to an unscrupulous family advisor. Laura cast the country's most popular and gifted actors in the lead roles. She strived to stage a witty and fluid production that would solidify her place among the theater greats as a quality manager and director. According to the February 26, 1859, edition of the *Boston Post*, "*Our American Cousin* is a delight and certainly turned the tide of popular favor in its direction winning affections of theatregoers everywhere."

Broadway-based theater managers recognized how financially viable the play was and a handful announced their intentions to produce the material. Laura was furious when she heard that the management at Barnum's Museum was going to stage *Our American Cousin*, and she sought a court order to stop them. Although she held an American copyright on the property the Supreme Court judge hearing the case ruled that Laura had no exclusive right to the material. It was ruled that the widow of Josh Silsbee, the man who cowrote the play with Tom Taylor, had the rights to the play. The judge's decision was later reversed.

Encouraged by John to continue on and still reeling from the judge's decision, Laura forged ahead with her own production of the now-controversial literary work. In February 1865 John Thompson Ford, owner of Ford's Theatre in Washington, invited Laura and her troupe to perform at his playhouse the second week of April. Ford had initially asked that Laura and her company perform a play about the temperance movement entitled *The Workmen*. The comedy had been another success for the actress and director, and Ford felt the material would work well with his audiences. Laura thought the theme of the production might be inappropriate to perform during the Christian Holy Week and suggested instead *Our American Cousin*. Ford agreed.

Laura was happy. Not only was her career doing well, but her relationship with John was solid. In early 1857 John had hired an attorney to quietly begin divorce proceedings against Laura's estranged husband. Not only was the divorce handled discreetly and without any newspaper coverage, the two had wed in 1860 in a secret ceremony at a justice of the peace's office in the Georgetown section of the District of Columbia. The couple was excited about the weeklong engagement at Ford's Theatre. On Friday, April 14, 1865, the pair attended an early mass before heading to the playhouse to begin the day's rehearsal and prepare for the night's show.

Among the many actors who came and went from the theater that day was John Wilkes Booth. He, too, was an actor, though many believed his brother Edwin to have possessed the true talent for theater. John Wilkes Booth had been employed at Ford's Theatre and frequently dropped by to check to see if any mail had been delivered there for him. He was such a regular at the theater no one thought his presence there to be out of the ordinary. He roamed about the playhouse at will, inspecting the sets, costumes, and box corridors and discussing the performances with fellow thespians. On April 14, John Wilkes Booth sat in on the rehearsal for *Our American Cousin*. He memorized the actors' parts and recited them aloud as he mulled over a plan he had for President Lincoln. President Lincoln was a man he had been vocal about disliking.

At 10:15 p.m. on April 15, 1865, John Wilkes Booth stood in the back of the theater surveying the audience. They were laughing and having a good time watching the play. No one noticed him walking down the hall to the stage box and closing the door quietly behind him. He quickly barred the door to prevent anyone from following him. In the darkness between the door he had just entered and the door of his destination, he drew his pistol. He heard the lines on stage and knew he had about two minutes.

When John Wilkes Booth heard one of the lead actors say, "Don't know the manners of good society, eh? Well, I guess I know enough to turn you inside out, old gal—you sock-dologizing old man-trap," he pushed open the door to President Lincoln's box and stood directly behind him. John Wilkes Booth fired the gun at the same time the crowd burst into laughter.

The afternoon after President Lincoln was shot and killed, Laura began packing to leave the city. She wanted as much distance between herself and the horrifying event as possible. She pleaded with her husband to collect the sets, costumes, and scenery from the production and send them to Cincinnati, where their next performance was to be held. The frightful calamity of the murder had shaken the usually composed actress and director to her core. All Laura wanted was for her life to return to normal, but law enforcement had other plans.

On April 17, 1865, Laura Keene was arrested at the train depot. According to the *Philadelphia Inquirer*, "She was bound for Cincinnati, accompanied by two actors named John Dyott and Harry Hacock." Many who worked at Ford's Theatre on the night of the assassination were arrested and held for questioning. John Wilkes Booth was an actor with ties to the theater and everyone associated with him or the performance of *Our American Cousin* was a suspect. The authorities even considered that Laura might have helped plan the shooting.

"She said she had given bail to appear in Washington," the *Philadelphia Inquirer* reported, "and had left owing to the excitement at the affair at the theatre. The whole three [meaning Laura and the two actors with her] are held by the military as a mere matter of precaution until the facts can be ascertained from Washington, when she will probably be discharged with apologies."

On April 19, 1865, Laura was released by order of the secretary of war. John was by her side to help her move beyond the tragic event and refocus on her theatrical ambitions. Laura canceled all future showings of *Our American Cousin* and replaced it with a play entitled *She Stoops to Conquer*. She then traveled to Cincinnati, where she and her company were scheduled to perform.

Laura struggled to lose herself in her work. About the time she thought the fog had lifted, someone, usually a fellow actress or a bold audience member, would ask her about the dress stained with President Lincoln's blood. Often fans would tug and pull at her clothes thinking the garment she was wearing was what she had on when she held the president's head in her lap.

John was mindful of how the very idea that she would ever wear that dress again was disturbing to his wife. The two discussed the matter at length and decided to ship the dress back to the designer in Chicago for him to dispose of however he wanted. John cut Laura's touring season and whisked her off to a remote and private residence in Riverside Lawn in Massachusetts.

John's health had begun to fail when Laura returned to the stage on a regular basis. For three years after the assassination, she was still unable to continue performing through an entire season without ministers and their church members grieving at the theater and berating her for what they perceived as the downfall of morals that led to the killing of President Lincoln. They blamed the theater and its artisans for the decay of society.

On April 18, 1869, John Lutz died of heart failure while visiting his brother in New York. He was fifty-four years old. He was buried in the family plot in Oak Hill Cemetery, Georgetown, next to his first wife, who was considered by elitists to be his only legal wife.

In the fall of 1869, Laura accepted an offer to manage the Chestnut Street Theatre in Philadelphia. She worked diligently on producing a series of new plays and for two seasons did not disappoint theatergoers. She toured the country with a stock company, performing plays she helped create. Both of Laura's grown daughters helped her write and stage the performances. The aging actress and director not only appeared in a variety of shows but also lent her talent to a lecture circuit and traveled to various cities sharing her knowledge of early theater.

On November 4, 1873, after more than twenty years in the theater, Laura passed away. News of her death was printed in papers from New York to London. According to the November 13, 1873, edition of the *Decatur Republican*, "Her loss will be deeply felt in the profession and also by the general theatre going public to whom her name is as familiar as a household word."

The November 10, 1873, edition of the *Boston Daily Globe* noted that Laura died from "consumption and exhaustion." Her personal physician informed the paper that "although she had been given the most modern medicine science could suggest . . . her constitution was broken." The doctor added he believed her "health had been on a decline since Lincoln's assassination."

Laura was buried at the Holy Angels Cemetery in Montclair, New Jersey.

Eleven months prior to Laura's passing she had sold *Our American Cousin* to actor E. A. Southern for $2,690. For this he received the rights for the United States and Canada plus the original manuscript.

*Our American Cousin* was performed numerous times between 1865 and 1872. Laura often wrote letters to theater managers protesting the use of material that she owned. She was most outraged with Edwin Booth when he produced his own version of the play a mere seven months after his brother had assassinated President Lincoln.

# Caroline Chapman

## The Quick-Change Artist

*We sincerely question if there ever was an actress more perfectly
at home upon the stage than Miss Chapman.*

—*DAILY ALTA CALIFORNIA*, SAN FRANCISCO,
MAY 24, 1853

The theater at Camp Seco, a gold camp in California, could
hardly compare to the Greenwich Street Theater in New
York, or the Jenny Lind in San Francisco, or theaters in New
Orleans, Philadelphia, or other cities she'd played in, but Caroline
Chapman had rarely seen a more enthusiastic audience. Twitching
her skirts into place, she waited for her cue. Tonight they would
conclude the program with a spoof of notorious entertainer Lola
Montez, an act that always brought down the house.

Caroline and her brother, "Uncle Billy" Chapman, had left
San Francisco in an uproar after starring in a hilarious play by Dr.
Robinson. Newspaper editors had sharp words for *Who's Got the
Countess?* and Caroline's part in it. How, they asked, could the
"modest" Miss Caroline Chapman descend to such tasteless, even
cruel burlesque of the lovely Lola?

That was easy, Caroline thought. She was a professional
actress, and as she waited for her cue, she could balance that accomplishment against a lack of beauty that had also been politely noted
in the press. Critics admired Lola's stunning face and form, but
few of them considered her a serious actress. Lola's stage career in
Europe had included a stint as the mistress of the King of Bavaria,

who had made her Countess of Landsfelt. Caroline, on the other hand, had started learning stage work as a child on her father's riverboat and had garnered praise from her first performance.

Beauty was not Caroline's stock in trade. Caroline was too plain to compete with the legendary Lola's charms. The most complimentary report on her appearance had come from theater historian Joseph Ireland, who described her as slender and plain featured but with excellent teeth in a large, mobile mouth. Her face was radiant with expression communicated by a pair of gleaming dark eyes that could convey more meaning, either of mirth or sadness, said Ireland, than any contemporary female on the New York stage.

Unlike the scandalous Lola, Caroline had never indulged in affairs with royalty or famous authors and had never smoked a cigar, kept a pet bear, or threatened to take a riding whip to a cynical newspaper editor. Caroline Chapman had what Lola lacked: talent. Nowhere did she find it more fun to exhibit than in Dr. Robinson's send-up of the glamorous Countess of Landsfelt, whose stage reputation depended more on her display of shapely legs than on a demonstration of acting ability.

Lola became famous for her Spider Dance—a frantic effort to shake blackened cork "spiders" from her skirts that required lifting and shaking of dress and petticoats—which shocked the polite world but attracted droves of admirers to the theater. Lola's well-attended appearances in San Francisco in 1853 inspired local theatrical entrepreneur Dr. G. C. Robinson to pen the hilarious farce *Who's Got the Countess?* in which Caroline performed. "Some weeks ago the Countess came to fill us with delight and drew admiring throngs to see her spider dance each night . . ." As Dr. Robinson's familiar song rang out over the heads of miners crowded into the makeshift theater, Caroline swirled haughtily onstage. She might not be beautiful, but she could act rings around the likes of Lola Montez.

Reviews showering praise on Caroline, Uncle Billy, and their repertoire filled newspapers across the state. The *Daily Alta California* in December 1853 reviewed Caroline's appearance at the American Theatre, noting that "she has never had an equal." The article concluded, "In either genteel or low comedy she far excels all others, and it matters not whether singing, dancing, or acting is required, she is equally proficient in all, and brings the highest cultivation and most graceful native qualities to the performances."

Born in 1818 into a dynasty of actors and producers who were famous at Haymarket and Covent Garden theaters in England, Caroline learned the acting craft in America after her father brought the family to New York. In 1831 Caroline's father, William Chapman, procured a large flatboat and turned it into a theater in which his family members were the players. Caroline started her career aboard Chapman's Floating Palace, the riverboat playhouse that may have been the first of its kind on the Mississippi. At about the age of eleven, Caroline stepped onstage to support the family's theatrical adventures at the American Opera House in New York.

The Chapman family was chock-full of actors, and the troupe plied the Mississippi for years before William Chapman died and many members of the family headed for the bustling streets of San Francisco. Caroline made her debut in New York as an adult in 1846. Her skills were favorably noted when she played in *A Husband at First Sight* at the age of twenty-eight at the Greenwich Street Theater.

She was thirty-two years old when she and her older brother, who became known as "Uncle Billy," arrived in San Francisco in 1850. According to some accounts, Uncle Billy may have been Caroline's father rather than her brother. Whatever the truth about their kinship, the duo became popular performers as soon as they hit the boards in the City by the Bay.

San Francisco was the jumping-off point for the goldfields. The sprawling territory of California was scarcely two years old, carried to statehood on the strength of the Gold Rush, which was luring thousands of young men from all over the world to the foothills of the Sierra Nevada. Many of these Argonauts were well educated and well traveled, and they knew their Shakespeare. Miners and the merchants who catered to them would line up outside a makeshift theater, dressed in their best, to buy an expensive ticket for a seat on a plank bench just to watch an itinerant troupe of actors perform *Hamlet* or *Romeo and Juliet*. If the show did not meet their expectations, the scruffy audiences were not above pitching ripe fruit at the players.

Caroline became an instant success with her first appearance in 1852 at Tom Maguire's imposing new Jenny Lind Theater, the third incarnation of the playhouse.

The first Jenny Lind Theater was built by impresario Tom Maguire on the floor above a gambling den called the Parker House Saloon in Portsmouth Square. In 1850 Maguire's first San Francisco theater had seemed a vast improvement over some others that were little more than rickety wooden structures, sometimes lacking a floor and roofed with canvas. Some barnstormers traveling between mining camps entertained in tents, saloons, and barns, with makeshift scenery and shoddy costumes.

By contrast, at the first Jenny Lind, patrons were enclosed within deep-rose wall panels, seated in gilded boxes from which they looked out on a painted drop curtain that was hung to set the scene.

Unfortunately all that splendor disappeared when, in May 1851, the Jenny Lind burned to the ground along with a large section of the city always prone to fire. Maguire immediately rebuilt and reopened on June 13; nine days later, however, only embers remained. Once again the indefatigable Maguire rebuilt, this time in a more permanent fashion.

Caroline Chapman

Caroline Chapman's first appearance in San Francisco was at the third, and most opulent, Jenny Lind Theater. The *Herald* said it was the "largest and handsomest building in the city." Built of brick with a white sandstone exterior imported from Australia, the new Jenny Lind was three stories tall and contained two thousand seats, including a balcony, galleries, opulent boxes, orchestra stalls, and a dress circle. Caroline's initial performance in late spring of 1852 was well received, and, during the remainder of the season, she showed her versatility in drama as well as farcical afterpieces.

Leaving the plush Jenny Lind behind in 1853, she and Uncle Billy made a tour of the mines. They were a smash hit from Nevada City to Sonora and points between. Although the weather was dismal at best, with torrential rains and heavy snowfall, the light-hearted actors brought sunshine and left with gold-lined pockets.

The Mother Lode region had something that made it an ideal venue for a popular actress: red-shirted miners hungry for entertainment, their "pokes" filled with spending money measured by the ounce. Gold dust in small leather bags landed with pleasing regularity at the feet of the actress following a performance.

The primitive stages in gold camps did not daunt this professional who had learned her craft in the small wooden structure nailed to her father's first flatboat theater. The editors of *A History of Tuolumne County* described the playhouse where the Chapman troupe played in 1853 as consisting of wood planks nailed together to make the walls, the whole covered by canvas, with, of course, a barroom through which patrons had to pass to reach the wooden benches placed before the stage:

> *In this primitive structure the Chapman Family held forth for many nights, playing the initial engagement. These actors seem to have had an exceedingly successful season in the mines, playing in all the camps which contained any facilities for such performances, or men enough to compose an audience. Every man went to hear*

*them, and very possibly no actors, "star" or otherwise, ever met the expectations of their audiences more fully; and certainly no audiences ever rose to the demands of the performers with such unanimity—such excess of satisfaction and ebullition of feeling—as theirs. At Columbia the stage was covered with buckskin purses, each containing what the generous givers thought a proper testimonial.*

According to the article, tossing pokes of gold at the feet of the company lacked the pleasing resonance the miners felt appropriate to the occasion. "Discovering, however, that there was not noise enough about it to fully emphasize their feelings, the boys took to throwing silver pieces, and there was, it was said, an immediate scarcity of these coins, which, by the way, had not long been in circulation."

The Phoenix Theater in Sonora advertised a grand opening on New Year's night with a full orchestra and a "powerful" company headed by Miss Caroline Chapman. It is said that more than a thousand miners acted as escort as the Chapmans traveled the five miles from Columbia to Sonora. Caroline delivered an opening address and then played with Uncle Billy in the three-act comedy *The Serious Family*, which was followed by dancing and singing. The program concluded with a favorite farce, *Rough Diamond*.

Following the triumphant and lucrative tour of the mines, in late 1853 Caroline returned to San Francisco where she continued to please audiences. Playing opposite the young Edwin Booth, Caroline displayed her talent well in a variety of roles. It was predicted that Edwin Booth would have an excellent career, based on his early years in San Francisco, but Caroline Chapman reached her zenith there.

In May 1853 the *Daily Alta California* noted her many virtues:

*In everything where versatility and tact can be displayed—where sprightly vivacity and laughing wit ap-*

*pear, singing, dancing, and acting are all required, she
probably has no equal on the American boards. There is
a laughing good humor evinced on all proper occasions,
which says, "I enjoy this, don't you?" in such a way that an
audience cannot help but be pleased from mere sympathy.
Everything of the light and airy kind she enters into with
that ease and freedom which seems to say that she is living
and not acting the character in which she appears.*

A benefit for the Union Grammar School in 1856 brought
Caroline to the stage in one of the plays that demonstrated her
unique abilities. In *The Actress of All Work*, she took on seven
different roles in rapid succession. The piece had always been a
favorite of audiences, since it showcased the quick-change talents
of the star. The *Daily Alta California* reported:

*As the country girl she was inimitable, and kept the house
in a perfect roar. As the high spirited actress she was
equally perfect, and the old woman was garrulous and
crack-voiced to the life. Then as the French danseuse she
showed that grace and agility which is often wanting in
many of those whose only merit is in their dancing and
who yet are accounted as great attractions at a theater.*

Since Lola Montez had lately displayed her talents as a dancer
in San Francisco, that veiled barb may have been aimed in the
flamboyant Lola's direction. Still, the Chapmans and Lola Montez
occasionally played the same bill, and Lola, despite her reputation
for horsewhipping editors who disparaged her talents, seemed
to ignore Dr. Robinson's spoof of her dancing. Members of the
public, however, sometimes came to Lola's defense. It was left to
a gentleman admirer to defend Lola's honor and chastise Caroline
in the *Herald*. At the end of his impassioned pleas to remember
the generosity of Lola Montez and cease attending the lampoon by
Dr. Robinson as performed by the Chapmans, the writer reminded
Caroline of her true calling:

*There probably never was, and never will be, an actress in San Francisco who has made more warm friends and admirers than Miss Caroline Chapman. She can play anything and do it well, and her name is an unfailing source of attraction wherever she appears. No matter what she undertakes, she renders herself acceptable and generally far more than acceptable to her audience. If she were to "play the Devil," I haven't the least doubt she would do it perfectly, and be greeted with roars of applause but we don't want to see any such character. Miss Chapman is a lady, and a most admirable artist; and I cannot believe that lowering her in this manner to a more profound depth than I had supposed low comedy to be capable of, can be any more agreeable to herself than it is to her admirers.*

The writer went on to beg Caroline to spurn the mockery of Lola Montez: "No! No! We've had enough of this; personalities may amuse for a moment, but a little reflection makes them offensive. Give us "BEAUTY" again, charming Carry, and don't let them make a Mule of you any longer."

"Charming Carry" apparently ignored the request and, by December 1853, was once again portraying a counterfeit "Countess" and keeping the audience in an uproar at the American Theatre.

Caroline, Uncle Billy, and other family members rented a large house atop one of San Francisco's fabled hills, and there they laughed and partied with friends and fellow thespians. Yet no breath of scandal about the popular actress was ever published in the newspapers in the city.

On New Year's Day 1862, another, and very surprising, notice appeared in the *Herald*. Under the headline "Elopement and Marriage," it was reported that Caroline Chapman had failed to appear onstage at the National Theatre to "take her part in the piece." The newspaper reported "the fair one could not be found." A Reverend Mr. Briggs reportedly married Caroline to a Mr.

Nichols, "well and favorably known in San Francisco." The story indicated Caroline's father had not approved of the match. There is at least one incorrect fact in the report. William Chapman Sr., who claimed Caroline as his daughter, had died in the 1840s, and the man some say was actually her father, "Uncle Billy" Chapman, died in 1857. No more is heard about Mr. Nichols, the groom, but Caroline continued to attract attention as an actress of considerable talent. Her career, however, slowly dwindled as the City by the Bay became enthralled with a variety of entertainment from melodeons (saloons with music-hall entertainment that included comedy, dance, and musical revues) to blackface minstrels to grand opera.

Caroline Chapman faded from the limelight as new, young actresses took to the boards in the vibrant city of San Francisco. By 1870 she was no longer performing. Perhaps it was the nature of the city, with its rapidly growing but transient population, that contributed to her descent into obscurity. Although the city had affectionately called her "Our Caroline" not many years before and newspapers had praised her for her modesty as well as her peerless skills as an actress, her *Daily Alta California* obituary noted only: "In this city, May 8th, Miss Caroline Chapman, from the City of London, aged 58 years."

# Jeanne Eagels

## The Screen Siren

*Superb actors do not grow on every bush.*

—JEANNE EAGELS, *NEW YORK TIMES,*
MAY 29, 1927

Actress Jeanne Eagels was an attractive, petite entertainer with delicate features. According to her friends and peers she was childish, adult, reasonable, unreasonable—usually one when she should be the other, but always unpredictable. The Oscar-nominated actress was born Amelia Jean Eagles on June 26, 1890, in Kansas City, Missouri. She was the second of four children born to Edward Eagles, a carpenter, and Julia Sullivan Eagles.* Edward and Julia were from Kentucky and both had an ancestry that could be traced back to France and Ireland.

As a child Jeanne was frail, but mischievous. There wasn't a boy on the block that wasn't afraid of her. According to the sole biography written about the famed thespian by Edward Doherty and entitled *The Rain Girl,* Jeanne was a tomboy. She liked to climb onto the roofs of barns, swing from the limbs of trees, walk fences, and skip from rafter to rafter in the attics of the buildings in the neighborhood.

"She was six or seven when she fell from a fence she and her sister were walking on," Doherty wrote about Jeanne. "She broke her right arm and ran home to her mother. A doctor was

---

* Jeanne changed her name from Eagles to Eagels when she signed on with the traveling troupe, because she thought it sounded better.

called, but he wasn't the best in the world. He set the arm, but it pained her all the rest of her life, especially when it was wet. And it was wet every night and every matinee for five years when Jeanne performed in her most recognizable stage role, that of Sadie Thompson in the play *Rain*." Throughout the duration of her career, Jeanne told newspaper and magazine reporters that she had broken her arm while traveling with the circus. She claimed she'd fallen off a white horse she was riding around the ring. It was the first of many stories she herself would contribute to the legend of Jeanne Eagels.

Jeanne made her stage debut at the age of eleven starring as Puck in *A Mid-Summer Night's Dream* at a drama school in Kansas City. From that moment on, she set her sights on a stage career and could not be persuaded to take anything else as serious as entertaining. She was educated primarily in public schools, but she never cared much for formal classroom settings and in 1905 dropped out of school completely.

Jeanne was fifteen when she took a job at a department store in a stock room earning five dollars a week. Before she turned sixteen, she had convinced a prominent Midwest casting agent to hire her to perform in vaudeville and tent repertoire shows as a bit player. Jeanne learned a great deal about theater as a part of the O. D. Woodward Stock Company and was equally adept at comedy and drama.

While working with the stock company, Jeanne met the Dubinsky Brothers, three actors and businessmen who ran a traveling melodrama troupe. Their careers, which began with the traveling tent shows, led to working on the silver screen and to building one of Kansas City's largest theater companies.** Jeanne was involved romantically with Maurice, the oldest of the Dubinskys. He signed Jeanne with their troupe, and she played

**The chain of theaters the Dubinskys founded is now known as AMC Theatres.

the heroine in a variety of shows opposite Maurice, who regularly performed as the villain.

Jeanne quickly became accustomed to the life of an intrepid actor and entertainer. Whether the venues where she and the troupe performed were regular opera houses with a stage and footlights, or a bare cold room over a grocery store with a row of kerosene lamps for footlights and only a wall to prop the scenery against, she relished the opportunity to appear before enthusiastic audiences. There were boys who whistled for virtue and triumphant and hissed the villain when there was dirty work afoot. There were also girls who sat pop-eyed and still all night and hardly breathed until the curtain fell. Jeanne loved them all and watched them from backstage.

In the spring of 1906, Jeanne married Maurice Dubinsky. He was her protector and mentor. He shared all of his acting ideas with her, gave her the best parts in his dramas, and saw to it that her name was featured on the playbills. Jeanne informed her family in Kansas City of the union months after the wedding had taken place. She was in Excelsior Springs, Missouri, on a belated honeymoon when she sent a wire about the nuptials. After a short celebration, Jeanne and the other members of the troupe continued with their tent show throughout the Midwest. By 1911, the Dubinskys were in New York. A great deal had happened in the five years they had been married. In addition to rehearsing and performing new plays in a series of venues in Iowa, Kansas, Oklahoma, Nebraska, and Illinois, the couple had had a child.

Whether the infant died at birth or Jeanne and Maurice gave him up for adoption is not clear. Fellow actors in the troupe, such as Ina Claire, shared with a reporter for *Liberty* magazine in 1929 that Jeanne told her that her son had passed away. Director Sam Forrest told reporters at *Liberty* magazine that Jeanne had shared with him that her child had not died but that Jeanne was too ashamed to

Jeanne Eagels

admit she'd let him be adopted. "I let people take him from me," Jeanne cried in 1910 during a rehearsal for the play *A Gentleman's Mother*. "I don't know whether he's dead or alive. I don't know whether he's a gentleman or a burglar. He may be a tramp and I would see him somewhere and would not recognize him."

Jeanne and Maurice divorced in late 1911. Friends of the couple speculated that their marriage was doomed once they decided to part with their son. "Neither was meant for parenthood," an anonymous source told a reporter for the December 23, 1939, edition of the *Ogden Standard-Examiner*. "Both were meant for careers. Jeanne must give herself only to the drama. Something in her would not let her quit the theatre. She was what she was, and she could not help it. She did not make herself. She could not change herself. She was an actress. And though she might have given birth, she could not be a mother."

Like many aspiring Broadway actresses, Jeanne worked with theatrical producer Florenz Ziegfield making thirty-five dollars a week portraying a character named Olga Cook in a play entitled *The Mind-the-Paint Girl*. Her part in a Ziegfield show led to other supporting roles in *The Crinoline Girl*, *The Professor's Love Story*, *Disraeli*, and *Hamilton*. *Hamilton* opened at the historic Knickerbocker Theatre, the first theater on Broadway to advertise its productions with electrical signs.

According to an article in the November 22, 1914, edition of the *Boston Daily Globe*, Jeanne's performance in *The Crinoline Girl* at the Colonial Theatre was "noteworthy" but paled in comparison to the performance she gave dramatic critic Edward Harold Crosby after the show. Crosby wrote in his column:

> *Jeanne Eagels is tall and willowy and has sunny hair and blue eyes. All this is very desirable, though not especially startling, yet Miss Jeanne Eagels is in many ways a remarkable young woman. In the course of our conversation, when she was dilating on her hopes and ambitions,*

*she made a statement that nearly caused me to fall off the chair in which I was sitting.*

*She said that she had long wished to become an actress and had studied hard to that end, but she had no inclination to play emotional roles. I do not recall another young woman on the threshold of professional life who expressed the same views. Tears and lamentations seem to be the goal of the majority, but here was one who thought it was preferable to bring sunshine and honest laughter, to lighten the burdens of life rather than augment them, and I wanted to assume a patriarchal attitude and observe, 'Verily, daughter, thou art wise beyond thy years!' I am quite convinced that Miss Eagels' originality will cause her to become a shining light in the profession in the immediate future.*

Audiences agreed with Edward Crosby and proved their admiration for Jeanne at theaters in the Southeast, where she toured in the comedic production of *Outcast*. The press called her acting "genius" and proclaimed that her "talent was of a rare type."

Between the launch of new plays, Jeanne kept company with wealthy businessmen who were infatuated with her and showered her with presents and provided her with an expensive posh apartment in which to live and automobiles and chauffeurs. One of the generous men was an associate with the financial house of Kuhn, Loeb & Co., now known as Shearson Lehman/American Express. According to Doherty's biography, Jeanne didn't care for the wealthy businessman, but she always accepted his gifts. Doherty wrote,

*The millionaire was but a glorified john, and Jeanne had learned how to handle johns of all sorts. This man could help her, not only financially but in many ways. He took her to shows and dinners, and gave parties for her to which he invited influential people. He introduced her to his banker and broker friends, and, listening to their talk and asking them questions, Jeanne learned more than most people ever learn about finance, though somebody else always had to take charge of her finances.*

When the run of *The Crinoline Girl* ended, Jeanne branched into film, lending her talent to the Thanhouser Company. The Thanhouser Company was one of the first motion picture studios in America, producing over a thousand silent films between 1909 and 1918. Jeanne initially found the work fascinating because it was different. She learned to act without an audience and without rehearsing. In the process she made new contacts and created new opportunities for herself. Her films, including *The Outcast* and *The House of Fear*, played throughout the United States and were particularly popular in Texas and New Mexico.

Jeanne returned to the stage in 1916 and 1917, starring in such plays as *The Great Pursuit, What's Your Husband Doing?*, and *The Laughter of Fools.* Her performances were well received, but she earned the most notoriety in that time with her role in *The World and the Woman.* The January 23, 1917, edition of *Newark Daily Advocate* praised Jeanne for her work and noted that her portrayal of a servant girl "clings to me constantly." "I am sure you do not fully realize the strength of the work you have done," the critic concluded in his review. The success of *The World and the Woman* prompted Thanhouser executives to quickly sign Jeanne to another motion picture.

Actors Clifton Webb and Willard Mack were instrumental in helping Jeanne advance in the theater. Willard, a playwright as well as a thespian, was taken with Jeanne from the moment he met her in late 1916. He was helping a friend cast a Broadway production when she came in to audition for a part. The two discussed Broadway and traveling tent shows, acting, and producers. Willard believed Jeanne had the potential to be the greatest living actress and promised to help her achieve that goal. Willard and Jeanne eventually became romantically involved. Her relationship with Clifton was never more than a deep abiding friendship. Clifton and Jeanne spent lots of time together. Along with Clifton's mother Mabel, the pair attended show openings, operas, and dinner parties.

Both Willard and Clifton encouraged Jeanne to appear in a feature film produced by the World Film Corporation entitled *The Cross Bearer*. Set in the Belgian city of Louvain during World War II, Jeanne portrayed the ward of the church cardinal in love with a Belgian officer. Her character wanted to marry the officer, but the German governor general desired to have her for himself. The film premiered on March 26, 1918, at Carnegie Hall, and audiences and critics praised the production and Jeanne's performance.

Before returning to the stage on September 9, 1918, in the comedy *Daddies*, Jeanne made two more films with the Thanhouser Company entitled *Fires of Youth* and *Under False Colors*. Jeanne enjoyed working onstage and in movies equally and was anxious to remain a part of both. The hours were long, but, according to her biographer Doherty, she loved it. Filming would begin early in the morning, and she would be finished in time for theater rehearsals or matinees. Years of performing in various shows and traveling with dramatic troupes prepared her for such a demanding schedule. Jeanne worked fourteen hours a day every day but Sunday.

In the summer of 1921, Jeanne traveled to Europe for a five-month stay. She was exhausted and had developed an addiction to sedatives she hoped to shake while abroad. Gossip columns from New York to San Francisco claimed Jeanne was going to Europe with Clifton Webb and that the two were to be married. According to the July 17, 1921, edition of the Sandusky, Ohio, newspaper *The Register*, the reporter wondered how Clifton was "able to cut through the ring of rich professional men and Apollos of the stage who surrounded Miss Jeanne Eagels and won her away from one and all of them." The articled continued,

> *Isn't Miss Eagels beautiful? Yes, indeed, she is—just look at her pictures. Successful? Eminently so. Couldn't she have married money? Well, of course. At least a dozen million-aires a year offered their names and fortunes to her. She*

*could have picked blindfolded out of them a husband who
would have given her a hundred thousand dollars a year
play money, a yacht, a flock of automobiles, jewels, a box at
the opera and all the other luxuries most women desire. A
husband who would have taken her, if she desired it, from
the more or less precarious position of the footlights, or, if
she did not desire it, could have lavished his wealth upon
safeguarding and perfecting her artistic career.*

*Can Mr. Webb, the dancer and actor, do all this?
Nothing like it. They will both now share the perils, ac-
cidents, surprises and precariousness of their profession.*

*Most women who are familiar with actor folk only
from the newspaper or from the theatre seats they buy will
marvel how Mr. Webb managed to overcome his bride-to-
be's natural womanly desire for all these gifts of wealth.
The stage folk themselves add to this same wonder another
point of view peculiarity that of the stage's own. Although
Mr. Webb has played many parts, nominally and techni-
cally he is only a dancer. And nowhere on earth is there
more caste than in the American theatre. The leading
woman is a very important individual. Her associates, if
she designs to have any, are the star or leading man or a
highly paid villain or some famed character actor.*

One of those whom Miss Eagels might have had was
Thomas L. Chadbourne, the millionaire corporation lawyer whom
President Wilson invited to join the commission that should adjust
the difference between labor and capital in this country, but did
not. He admired the beauty and the talent of the young Western-
risen star. His magnificent limousine carried her daily to the theatre in which she was appearing.

When Miss Eagels was preparing to play the leading role
in *The Wonderful Thing*—the wonderful thing being love—the
astute lawyer sat watching the evolution of dramatic order out of
the chaos of first rehearsals. The bumps on the way to perfecting troubled, pretty Miss Eagels. She became acutely nervous.
One especially wearing afternoon she sank sobbing to the floor
of the stage.

She sobbed once or twice and fainted! Had Mr. Chadbourne been an actor or athlete he would have leaped from the orchestra to the stage. Being a dignified man of the law he walked hastily around behind the stage box and hurried to the side of the stricken beauty. He lifted her in his arms and carried her to the star's dressing room. There smelling salts and a glass of ice water quickly revived her.

"I'm so sorry and ashamed," she said when her strength returned.

Whether Miss Eagels meant she was sorry and ashamed because she fainted or because Mr. Chadbourne hadn't leaped like a goat like William S. Hart over the rails and the gaping gap of the auditorium upon the stage was not known. At any rate, soon after this the multi-millionaire gave up hope of making the star his own leading lady.

There were many others who pursued for a time and then gave up the chase. When attractive and unattached or otherwise leading men played ardent love scenes with her there was speculation as to whether they could withstand the allure of her remarkable beauty and her high-power magnetism plus propinquity. Broadway audiences and players speculated on the outcome when Cyril Scott, as the villain, made fervent love to her in a recent successful melodrama at the one-time millionaire's theatre, the Century.

Mr. Scott shortly afterward faced tragedy in hideous form when his wife, after twenty years of happy marriage, hanged herself in their home at Bayside, Long Island. They speculated too, these super-sophisticated playgoers and playmakers and players, when handsome Bob Warwick, distinguished soldier and actor, as her stage husband, played his scene of maddened love and jealousy with her in a recent success.

They speculated while dancer and actor Clifton Webb smiled, that from the moment of that meeting he thought her dark and calling eyes had held a promise of happiness for him. Mr. Webb thought right—despite the handicaps against him.

Jeanne Eagels is still very young. If it takes her no longer to win success for Clifton Webb than it did for herself, and if her romance with the dancer and actor is no more lengthy than many Broadway romances are, there may yet be time for her to marry wealth and high social position, as such a surprising number of her fellow stage stars have done.

When Miss Eagels sailed to Europe a few days ago Mr. Webb and his mother were on the same ship. The marriage, Broadway's informed and informers say, may occur in Paris or in Madrid, according to Miss Eagels.

> *Clifton and his mother Mabel did indeed travel to Europe on the same ship with Jeanne, but there was no plan to marry. In addition to taking a much-needed rest, Jeanne was also hoping the many creditors to whom she owed money would forget her debts while she was away. According to Clifton and Mabel Webb, Jeanne spent or gave away most all the money she earned. She showered herself, friends, and family with gifts on a regular basis, and paying bills was unimportant to her. Whenever she found herself lacking funds, she would become involved with wealthy businessmen who would support her as long as she allowed. Such was the case with the rich Italian entrepreneur Jimmie Auditore, who escorted her to Europe.*

Jimmie fell in love with Jeanne after seeing her in the films she made. The fact that he was married with children was of complete indifference to Jeanne after a while. Jimmie, an influential man with dubious connections, aggressively pursued Jeanne. He sent her tubs of orchids, a variety of jewelry, and furs. Initially she returned his gifts and boldly announced she wanted nothing to do with him. It wasn't until Jimmie presented Jeanne with a coffin made of brocaded silks and satins with handles of ivory and solid gold and containing an abundance of flowers that she relented.

The note that accompanied the intimidating gift read, "Love me or lie among the flowers." Their romance was brief and only ended once they returned from overseas and Jeanne announced publicly how much she hated him.

An article in the January 13, 1922, edition of *The Lima News* read,

> *When fascinating Jeanne Eagels tripped down the gang-plank of a transatlantic ship news reporters gave her an appreciatively squint, noted the latest cuts in Paris skirts, and then asked one another why Miss Eagels somehow seemed different. It wasn't her face, pink and piquant as ever. It wasn't her manner, or her chic frock, or her dashing hat. The ship's news sleuths observed that Miss Eagels, famous for wearing shimmering jewelry, was not wearing a single bauble. Just before sailing to Europe, she dazzled those on board the ship with her gorgeous diamond rings and her expensive, diamond necklace.*
>
> *Further inquiries into the unique situation revealed that she was wearing no such jewelry when she went through customs upon returning to the United States. According to rumors among the ship's passengers, Jeanne's rings were crushed and her necklace was missing all together. And there the story might have died if the notion of those crushed rings and the missing necklace hadn't persistently piqued the curiosity of the ship news gang. And when the ship news began to interview a few of the people who crossed to France with Jeanne Eagels they unearthed a sea mystery of the Flying Dutchman or any other ocean legend and much more romantic.*
>
> *They located the necklace after a fashion. It is somewhere at the cozy bottom of the Atlantic or adorning a mermaid, or reposing in the lining of some fish not too choosy about his diet. And they confirmed what happened to the rings. It was feet—feet furiously jumping up and down—that cracked them and crushed them and ground them into the promenade deck of the steamship.*
>
> *But what the ship's news reporters can't find out and what a lot of Broadway gossipers would like to know is who*

*plucked the necklace from Miss Eagels' slim throat and flung it forty fathoms deep, and whose feet performed the clog on Miss Eagels' other sparkles?*

*Miss Eagels, it is established, was the center of a gay little group about the ship. There was Clifton Webb, the dancer and actor, Clifton Webb's mother, and Louise Goody, another Broadway star. And there was also sailing at the last minute Jimmie Auditore, New York's million- aire stevedore, as buff and democratic as when he used to shove banana crates along the East River docks before he built his fortune out of the business.*

*One evening Miss Eagels decided to take a stroll on deck. Just what happened above decks then only the stars and the sea know. Unless you count Miss Eagels and the mysterious owner of the hands and feet that did such dreadful things to all her Tiffany pretties. But, below decks a few minutes later did happen, according to the passengers on the ship.*

*Louise was in her suite preparing for bed when she heard someone outside the passage and then someone pounding heavily on her door. She quickly answered it to find Miss Eagels on the other side. Her hair was mussed, cheeks burning, and eyes blazing. Apparently, Miss Eagels had been arguing with Jimmie Auditore. "The brute— the brute!" She could be heard saying. "He grabbed me like I was a sack of something and jerked the necklace right off my neck and threw it overboard! He threw it overboard—my diamond necklace! Oh dear—the brute! And he jerked my rings off my fingers and threw them and stamped on them."*

*The slam of a door muffled the monologue just when it was getting most interesting, and though Louise's neigh- bors almost split their ears straining they got nothing af- ter that but a low murmur. And that was all the ship's reporters got too when they began their little investiga- tion. And there the story rests while the necklace rests at the bottom of the sea."*

On January 21, 1921, Jeanne opened on Broadway at the Century Theatre in a play called *In the Night Watch*. Critics called her performance as a captain's wife "persuasive" and "riveting."

The following year Jeanne was offered a part in a play that would solidify her place among the finest stage actresses on Broadway. The part was of a harlot in South America who meets a missionary who tries to reform her. The character's name was Sadie Thompson and the play was *Rain*. A review in the December 10, 1923, edition of the *San Francisco Chronicle* extolled the virtues of Jeanne's brilliant presentation and in so doing inadvertently listed the parallels between the actress and the part she played:

> *She neglects nothing that adds a light by which to judge Sadie—that tender little bit on the old sofa that brings memories of her home in Kansas, for instance. How lovingly she fingers the woodwork, as she perhaps had done hundreds of times as a child, and all the while, she is talking flippantly to a crowd of men around her, trying to make an impression.*
>
> *A shallow creature, this Sadie, untaught, hard from the knocks she has received at the hands of the world, a good deal of a child for all her worldly wisdom, hating men for their treatment of her, but using them to such pleasure out of life as it holds for her, impudent and loose of tongue, an enticing little devil, choice enough to tempt even the anchorite, Reverend Dawson. Miss Eagels makes her all these things, and adds her own vibrant subtle feminine personality to make a magnificent creation of this wanton from the purlieus of Honolulu.*

"*Rain* is a powerful drama, wonderfully moving for all its occasional brazen ugliness and unyielding realism," an article in the November 26, 1922, edition of the *Salt Lake Tribune* noted, "and amazingly well acted by Jeanne Eagels as Sadie Thompson. It is another of those flashing hits common to our stage in which an impassioned ingénue tears smugness and hypocrisy to tatters and exits amid the tumultuous shouts of sympathetic audience. Miss Eagels carries her scenes perfectly."

In addition to a wealth of accolades, the thirty-nine-year-old Jeanne reaped healthy financial rewards from the success of

*Rain.* With the well-earned income, she purchased a large home in Westchester County, New York.

Clifton and Mabel Webb helped Jeanne settle into her new home but recognized she was melancholy and pensive. The mood was unexpected. She was a star, the greatest actress in the world. She had reached the heights, and all her ambitions had been realized. The Webbs anticipated that Jeanne would be happy that all her dreams of glory had come true, but instead she was the exact opposite. She had taken up smoking when she began rehearsing *Rain* and began drinking whiskey as the show began the second season on Broadway in mid-November 1923. The smoking and drinking increased after meeting Heisman Trophy winner Ted Coy and wealthy patron of the arts Whitney Warren Jr. Both men were romantically involved with Jeanne, and both were married or engaged to others when they began keeping company with the actress.

According to the December 23, 1923, edition of the *Ogden Standard-Examiner*, Whitney's parents didn't approve of his relationship with Jeanne, but theirs was not the first romance the Warrens had disapproved. The newspaper reported,

> *The course of the romance for Mr. Whitney Warren, Jr. apparently is not the joyous and triumphant affair one would expect for such a forceful and good-looking young hero and one who comes of such a rich and in every way distinguished family. Whether it is some heiress of fashionable society or some charming genius of the stage on whom he sets his heart, there seems always to be a stern parental hand to reach out and seize the young man by the coat collar and drag him firmly away from the object of his devotion.*
>
> *He falls in love only to be promptly yanked out again and the deeper he falls the more vigorous the restraining and restoring yank of what is suspected to be a watchful father's hand. At least this is how it looks to an envious public, which is beginning to find richer food for gossipy*

*speculation in Whitney Warren's troubled love affairs than it has found in any other young man's in a long time.*

*Whitney Warren won the heart of Geraldine Miller Graham, the California heiress, when the Prince of Wales pronounced the most superbly charming of any of the American beauties with whom he has danced and flirted. The engagement was announced with all the formality fashionable society demands. And then, after the anticipated brilliant wedding had been postponed for months came the news that it would never take place—that the engagement had been broken by mutual consent.*

*The real truth of the matter, however, is believed to be that the hero was yanked out of the love match by a parental hand. The Warrens are thought to have decided that Miss Graham was not the right bride for him. Whitney Warren plunged into theatrical work. He became connected to the brightest star of all—Jeanne Eagels. She is an actress who has risen from humble trouping with "Uncle Tom's Cabin" companies to one of the most admired and also one of the most sternly criticized roles on New York's Broadway.*

*Very soon it began to be whispered that the young aristocrat who had been unable for some mysterious reason to marry the fashionable Graham heiress was showing in Miss Eagels a much deeper interest than ordinarily would be expected from an employer of a theatrical firm with the actress whom many think its greatest star.*

*The whispers of gossip soon grew to shouts of positive belief that the romance had already reached the point of a secret engagement and that they would be married early next spring. The young man's father, Whitney Warren, the noted architect, flatly denied that any engagement existed between his son and the actress. The young man himself declined to discuss the matter. Miss Eagels? Well, the reporters were unable to reach her.*

*The mother of Miss Eagels, living in a fashionable home just a few doors from New York's most fashionable avenue, denied the report that she had already planned a great party to celebrate the engagement of her actress daughter to the wealthy architect's son. Three denials and refusals to confirm or deny and reports of hearty laughter only strengthened the theories of the gossip. As they well know from experience with many romances, this is quite the way it always is when some son of the smart set falls in love with some beauty of the stage.*

*Whatever the objection the Whitney Warrens might have had to Geraldine Graham might easily be multiplied in the case of Jeanne Eagels. Whatever her accomplishments are on stage it is speculated that her success does not make her a desirable candidate for a daughter-in-law. It is strongly suspected that such a prejudice is responsible for the reported effort of the Warren parental hand to yank the son and heir out of another relationship.*

When the relationship between Jeanne and Whitney reached the conclusion his parents had hoped, Jeanne was left to focus all her attention on Ted. Ted's wife, Sophia, filed for divorce over the affair, leaving the couple free to marry. Sophia threatened to smear the athlete's name in the press if he didn't relinquish his rights to his two sons. Outraged by the suggestion, Jeanne hired a private detective agency to look into the woman's background. The detectives learned that Ted's wife was a mistress of a powerful, well-known banker. The banker proved to have more influence over the press than Jeanne and was not only able to suppress information about the affair with Sophia but also arranged to have articles written about Jeanne and Ted's relationship. Sophia was granted the divorce based on the grounds of desertion and was awarded custody of the children.

Ted Coy loved Jeanne Eagels; she may have loved him as she claimed, but their marriage, which occurred in August 1925, in Bay Ridge, Connecticut, was a catastrophe for both. Their union began in scandal, and the press did everything they could to cast the two in a bad light. The couple struggled financially, too. The divorce had drained Ted of the majority of his funds, and Jeanne was fiscally irresponsible with every dime she earned. To offset

Jeanne Eagels poses for a photo to promote the film *The Letter*

the rumors that the newlyweds were living entirely off of Jeanne's earnings, Ted proposed that he become Jeanne's manager. In that capacity he could earn a living and feel less humiliated about the way he was getting by. Jeanne refused to hire him. She didn't like the idea of being managed by anyone.

In addition to the financial issues, the pair was socially imbalanced as well. Ted had trouble connecting with the theatrical personalities who were friends with Jeanne. He had little in common with them, and although his wife's associates were kind to him, Ted didn't fit in and was uncomfortable most of the time.

Jeanne's drinking became a major stumbling block in her new marriage. She often drank to excess and would pick those times to air the couple's marital troubles. She made a scene in restaurants, at premier parties, and press events. Ted would do his best to control her outbursts, but she would slap him if she felt he was trying to rule over her. As time went on, Ted decided to remain behind at Jeanne's farm in upstate New York rather than travel with his wife where she was performing. He decided not to go with her when she was on tour with *Rain* and the play that followed entitled *The Garden*. Ted was faithful to pay Jeanne's bills when she sent money home, but all too often she did not send money home. Prohibition was in full swing, but Jeanne always managed to find a party where alcohol was being served. She generally bought rounds of drinks for everyone at speakeasies she frequented.

Although Jeanne never missed a rehearsal or a performance because of her drinking, the effect of the overindulgent life she was living was reflected in the way she looked. She was pale and listless; the show's directors accused her of looking "half-dead." The producer of *Rain* demanded that an understudy be hired in case something happen to the spirited actress. Jeanne threw a fit and refused to continue with the play at all if an understudy was hired. The producer gave into Jeanne's demand. "Maybe I am half-dead," she told the director and producer, "but I'll always be able to play Sadie Thompson." True to her word, Jeanne never failed to appear as Sadie. She played the character of Sadie for five years on Broadway and on the road to theaters in San Francisco. During that time she missed only eighteen performances due to illness.

In late 1926 Jeanne was cast as Roxie Hart in the play *Chicago*. The numerous arguments she had with the play's director led to her dismissal from the role, and Francino Larrimore, rising star and stunning French-Italian beauty, was given the lead instead.

The January 2, 1927, edition of the *Oakland Tribune* reported that the reason Jeanne was not starring in the production was because she was "engrossed in the business of divorcing her husband." Ted Coy and the tempestuous actress were indeed on the verge of ending their union. Jeanne told anyone who would listen that Ted was physically abusive. In February 1926, a bruised and battered Jeanne was spotted by a friend checking into the Hotel Sherman in New York. When the friend asked what had happened, Jeanne remarked that Ted had broken her jaw. The true story about what really happened wouldn't be divulged until late 1929.

Between losing the part in *Chicago* and dissolving her marriage to Ted, Jeanne performed on Broadway in a comedy entitled *Her Cardboard Lover*. Critics were pleased to see Jeanne embrace a role other than that of Sadie Thompson. A notice in the March 27, 1927, edition of the *Lima News* read that it "relieves the fear that Jeanne might have clung forever to her old hit, *Rain*." Owing to bad reviews, *Her Cardboard Lover* did not linger long onstage. Once the show closed, Jeanne traveled to Los Angeles to star in a picture with John Gilbert called *Man, Woman, and Sin*. Produced by Metro-Goldwyn-Mayer, Jeanne played a newspaper editor who falls in love with a cub reporter devoted to his mother. The silent film was a commercial success and audiences were "amazed by the portrayal of what goes on behind the scenes in the newspaper world." Moviegoers called Jeanne's performance "sweet" and "charming."

Behind the scenes of *Man, Woman, and Sin*, Jeanne was anything but sweet and charming. According to Doherty, Jeanne hated everyone on the studio lot except the director and her leading man. She was irritable and hard to get along with, and the supporting players in the picture with her noted that she now "found the entire movie making process boring."

At one point during the filming, Jeanne walked off the set and didn't return for three days. Studio officials complained that it was her drinking that caused problems. It was rumored in Hollywood that Jeanne had to be propped up and held while the cameraman shot her close-ups and that a double was used whenever possible to speed up the filming. Jeanne's friends and family blamed her drinking large quantities of champagne on the fact that she was humiliated by her impending divorce.

In February 1928 the marriage between Jeanne Eagels and Ted Coy was legally terminated. The courts granted Jeanne a divorce based on the grounds of extreme cruelty. By August 1928 Ted had remarried. His third wife was Lottie Bruhn of El Paso, Texas. According to the August 16, 1928, edition of the *Laredo Daily Times*, "The twenty-one year old bride was a college girl whose father was a wealthy, retired businessman."

Producers of the play *Her Cardboard Lover* had reworked the play and were taking the show on the road in March 1928, and Jeanne was the star of the traveling troupe. The play was to open in Milwaukee. The Milwaukee Press Club had bought out the house for every night in the week and sold thousands of dollars' worth of advertising for the program. Unfortunately Jeanne Eagels was a no-show, and there was no understudy on whom to fall back. The cast and crew spent days looking for the actress. They searched every speakeasy between Chicago and Milwaukee. She was finally located at the Congress Hotel in Chicago, ill and very drunk.

The manager of the theater in Milwaukee, along with the troupe's company manager, persuaded Jeanne to come with them to Milwaukee, but she refused to leave her hotel room once she arrived. She insisted that she was extremely ill and that alcohol was not the cause of her sickness. Doctors examined Jeanne and found that she had a throat infection and was suffering from exhaustion. The theater manager refused to believe the physician's diagnosis. He was convinced that Jeanne's problem was that she drank too much champagne, and he therefore demanded something be done about the financial hardship she had caused him. He took his demand to the Actor's Equity, the labor union that represented actors and stage managers.

Once it was announced by representatives of Actor's Equity that some action would be taken against Jeanne, the May 6, 1928, edition of the *San Antonio Light* featured an article about the temperamental actress's situation and asked if the union could cure Miss Jeanne Eagel of "staritis." The article read,

> It was a bitter pill that the actor's union made the actress swallow, but, then "staritis" is an awful thing to have and it is catching. Stage temperament is different. All stars are supposed to get that. It is a sort of occupational disease of the theatre that comes on as soon as an actor sees his name in electric lights. As long as the symptoms are confined to emotional outbursts at rehearsals and in the manager's office, nobody minds much, but when it gets so bad that it closes a show and throws a whole company of actors out of work, that is serious, and Broadway calls it "staritis."
>
> Miss Eagels caused a great deal of problems because of her absence. Days passed, the theatre remained dark, the company idle, the management began to tear its hair, already made gray by the erratic star. Here was a hit losing more money than the worst failure because its much advertised star was lost somewhere in the depths of Chicago. Someone suggested that she might have been kidnapped by gunmen.
>
> Toward the end of the week the lady of mystery turned up with the simple explanation that she hadn't been feeling well. Genius is supposed to be simple and so is Miss Ea-

*gels sometimes. It was too late to do anything in Milwaukee, but there was a fine advance sale in the next town, St. Louis. So the manager bought flowers for the star and the company took turns petting and pitying her and asking no questions. Such perpetual adoration usually will soothe even the most impossible prima donna and all might have been well if the Equity had not heard of these strange actions and sent a representative from Chicago to see why a good actress was apparently turning into a "bad actor."*

Equity's main business is to see that actors get all that is coming to them from the managers, but it also undertakes to police its own members to the extent of making them have some regard for contracts. With her usual simplicity, Miss Eagels refused to see the Equity delegate, but it didn't settle the matter anymore than refusing to see a policeman. Also, his call seems to have made the star indisposed again and when the company went to St. Louis she simply did not choose to go with them. The manager knew where she was this time, but it didn't do him any good.

In despair the management brought the company back to New York, paid it off and called the attention of the Equity to the losses caused by the charming actress. The thespian union summoned Miss Eagels to appear before the council of twenty-five members to determine just what had gotten into her. They read a long list of charges, most of which have not been made public. The actress explained the snubbing of the union's plenipotentiary by stating that she didn't think she was a genuine representative. This excuse would not go very well with a traffic cop and it didn't go well with the Equity either. To justify her remaining in Chicago when she should have been in Milwaukee and in Milwaukee when she should have been in St. Louis, thereby wrecking the show, she offered in evidence certificates from twelve doctors which stated that she had been "too ill to work."

The documents were greeted with a sad smile. Every time Equity asks an actor where he has been he flashes one of these medical alibis. They seem to be about as easy to get as one for a pint of rye. However, the council was inclined to agree that she was far from a well woman and needed treatment. The diagnosis of the committee was "staritis"

*in its most aggravated form and all being actors they*
*ought to know. It was a verdict of a jury of her peers.*

Equity representatives finally decided to fine Jeanne thirty-six
hundred dollars for her actions and also banned her from the stage
for eighteen months. Their findings were announced on April 6,
1928.

Jeanne retreated to her home in Ossining, New York. She
eventually joined a vaudeville show and toured the northeast. It
was a triumph for her. She was a headliner wherever she went.
According to Doherty, "She drank more than ever after the show
and kept a supply of liquor in her dressing room." Jeanne was not
always drinking alone. She kept company with actor Barry O'Neill,
business owner Jack Colton, and many other men who coveted
her attention. The offer to make talking pictures for Paramount
in mid-1928 inspired her to remain sober for a time. She took a
hiatus from romance while she was filming as well.

Jeanne's lucrative movie contract included three films, *The
Letter*, *Jealousy*, and *The Laughing Lady*. She would only be able
to make two of the pictures, because her health was failing. Her
throat infection had never been cured, and she had been diagnosed with neuralgia and kidney disease. More and more drugs
were needed to help her sleep and then be revitalized. Despite
her physical issues, she delivered stellar performances, particularly
in *The Letter*. Jeanne played a bored and restless housewife who
shoots and kills the man with whom she is having an affair. She
received an Academy Award nomination for best actress for her
performance.

Jeanne struggled with her eyesight while she was making
*Jealousy*. She had ulcers on her eyes and needed an operation to
correct her vision, but she didn't want to take the time to bother
with it. She drank to cope and frequently forgot her lines. The
film crew had to write her dialogue on a blackboard so she could

read them as she performed. Depending on her mood, she would either read the lines as written or make up whatever lines came into her head.

According to Jeanne's biographer, she loved her performance in *The Letter* but hated *Jealousy*, because she believed so many of her best scenes had been cut out. "I have grown to hate the movies," she reportedly told a friend. "They're stupid. They're inane. I want to go back to the stage." Audiences loved to see Jeanne wherever they could. The August 25, 1928, edition of the *Kingston Gleaner* noted that "her beauty and talent are brilliant both on stage and in films." The May 12, 1929, edition of the *Salt Lake Tribune* also boasted of the actress's popularity and the devoted fans she had in all walks of life. "Jeanne Eagels, disciplined by Equity, was barred from the stage and life looked exceedingly dark for her until along came *The Letter*," the report read. "Today she is known in small towns and hamlets that had never heard of the name Jeanne Eagels before. In spite of an unfortunate temperament and a strong tendency to do what she pleases, she is today highly regarded as a screen actress and her public adores her. The movies certainly came into Miss Eagels life at the best psychological moment, if you pardon the banality."

There were times Jeanne's fans got too carried away with their affection for her. In late May 1929, she had to hire a private detective because a moon-eyed youth was calling her home on a constant basis and even laid in wait for her in the lobby of the hotel where she was staying. The man was eventually arrested.

In September 1929 Jeanne announced that she was going to abandon film work indefinitely because she found it "wholly unsatisfying." Her plan was to take a break from work until the forced hiatus Equity had imposed was lifted. She would travel back and forth from her Park Avenue apartment to her farm in Ossining, reading plays and considering which project she wanted to do next. She continued to drink heavily and frequented speakeasies in the evenings.

On Thursday, October 3, 1929, Jeanne had breakfast with her secretary at her apartment, and the two women then discussed gowns and what they would wear at the opening of a new night club that weekend. Not long after Jeanne's secretary left, Jeanne received a call from Barry O'Neill. She informed him that she was going to her home in Westchester County for a few days. By mid-afternoon Jeanne had become violently ill and had asked her chauffer to take her to the hospital. The thirty-nine-year-old actress died shortly after arriving at the private sanitarium on Park Avenue.

The theatrical world was shocked by Jeanne's passing. The *Ogden Standard-Examiner* was just one of many papers that reported the news about her death and the results of the autopsy. The autopsy was performed by Dr. Thomas A. Gonzales, assistant chief medical examiner. The October 4, 1929, edition of the *Ogden Standard-Examiner* noted that the cause of death was alcoholic psychosis. "It's the same old story, nothing unusual," Dr. Gonzales said. "Miss Eagels died of alcoholism, not acute alcoholism, but from alcoholic psychosis."

An article in the October 7, 1929, edition of the *Thomasville Times-Enterprise* read,

> *Jeanne Eagels was a star. We are always learning that the success of a star depends more on the life she leads than on her stage effects. Jeanne was weak lamentably so. She was an enemy to her career and debauched herself to the extent that her usefulness quickly ended. Death came as a result of alcoholic poison and the resultant use of sleep potions to drive away the nightmares that are its final symptoms.*
>
> *Poor woman. She strove for happiness perhaps, but went the wrong path to get it. She did not have the fine qualities of a true woman nor could she curb an appetite that has bound her until death. So it is with many of the flutterbirds of the stage and screen. They think they can go the paces, drink unceasingly and then come back strong the next night for the performance. The physical strain is too great, the mental stress too keen and the result is a*

*disabled body and a weakened mind. So ends the chapter*
*of another of the brilliant victims of the demon rum.*

According to the October 7, 1929, edition of the *Oakland Tribune*, Jeanne Eagels's body was returned to Kansas City, Missouri, to be laid to rest. Her mother, two brothers, and sister planned the actress's funeral service, which was attended by more than three thousand people including many Broadway and Hollywood stars. Among those stars were Clifton Webb and Barry O'Neill.

Ted Coy wept when he heard that Jeanne had passed away. He was further grieved when he heard that one of the four rings she was wearing when she died was the diamond wedding ring set with seven diamonds and a pearl that he had given her. Months after her passing, Ted shared with newspaper reporters that the broken jaw and bruises she had when he was married to Jeanne were the result of a fall she had taken on a train when she was drunk. "She hit her head on the sink in our passenger car," he told reporters. "She'd had too much whiskey and fell over trying to make it to the bathroom."

Jeanne Eagels is buried at the Calvary Cemetery in Kansas City, Missouri.

# Bibliography

## General Sources
### Newspapers

*Argonaut,* Los Angeles, June 16, 1877.

*Argonaut,* Los Angeles, March 7, 1898.

*The Californian,* Salinas, November 4, 1848.

## Books/Magazines/Historical Quarterlies

Chinoy, Helen Krich and Linda Walsh Jenkins, eds. *Women in American Theatre.* New York: New York Theatre Communications Group, Inc., 1987.

Curry, Jane K. *Nineteenth-Century American Women Theatre Managers,* Lanham, MD: Rowman and Littlefield, 1994.

Gagey, Edmond M. *The San Francisco Stage, A History.* New York: Columbia University Press, 1950.

Furman, Evelyn E. Livingston. *The Tabor Opera House, A Captivating History.* Denver, CO: Self-published (Library of Congress Catalogue Number 72-88027), 1972.

James, Edward T., Janet Wilson James, and Paul S. Boyers, eds. *Notable American Women 1607–1950.* Cambridge, MA: Belknap Press of Harvard University Press, 1971.

Leman, Walter M. *Memories of an Old Actor.* San Francisco: Roman Co., Publishers,1886.

MacMinn, G. R. *The Theater of the Golden Era in California.* Caldwell, ID: The Caxton Printers, Ltd., 1941.

Marryat, Frank *Mountains and Molehills: Recollections of a Burnt Journal.* New York: J. B. Lippincott Company, 1855.

Robinson, Alice M., Vera Mowry Roberts, and Milly S. Barranger, eds. *Notable Women in the American Theatre, A Biographical Dictionary.* New York: Greenwood Press, 1989.

Rourke, Constance. *Troupers of the Gold Coast.* New York: Crowell Publishing Co., 1928.

Smith, Sean W. *A Woman's Role: Gender and the Legitimate Theatre in Gold Rush San Francisco, 1848–1856.* Ann Arbor, MI: UMI Company Ann Arbor, 1999.

# Mary Anderson
## Newspapers

*Daily Alta California,* San Francisco, April 4–16, 1876.

*Daily Alta California,* San Francisco, August 20–27, 1876.

*Daily Alta California,* San Francisco, August 5, 1886.

*Daily Alta California,* San Francisco, August 27, 1886.

*Oakland Tribune,* June 9, 1940.

*Sacramento Bee,* April 3, 1886.

*San Francisco Call,* May 19, 1891.

*San Francisco Chronicle,* February 27, 1903.

*San Francisco Chronicle,* April 1, 1903.

*San Francisco Chronicle,* May 22, 1921.

## Books/Magazines/Historical Quarterlies

Anderson, Mary. *A Few Memories.* London: Osgood, McIlvaine & Co., 1896.

Anderson, Mary. *A Few More Memories.* London: Hutchinson & Co., 1936.

*The Grizzly Bear Journal.* Los Angeles, California September 1907.

# Sarah Bernhardt
## Newspapers

*Anaconda Standard,* Anaconda, MT, September 23–27, 1891.

*Anaconda Standard,* Anaconda, MT, April 25, 1906.

*Anaconda Standard,* Anaconda, MT, May 6, 1906.

*Argonaut,* San Francisco, May 21, 1881.

*Argonaut,* San Francisco, January 4, 1897.

*Butte Miner,* Butte, MT, February 27, 1921.

*Montana Standard,* Butte, MT, March 27, 1903.

*Montana Standard,* Butte, MT, May 7, 1978.

*San Francisco Call,* May 10, 1887.

*San Francisco Call,* May 16, 1887.

*San Francisco Call,* May 17, 1887.

*San Francisco Call,* April 14, 1891.

*San Francisco Call,* April 25, 1891.

*San Francisco Call,* September 6, 1891.

*Seattle Post–Intelligencer,* September 25, 1891.

## Books/Magazines/Historical Quarterlies

*American Heritage,* Rockville, MD, July/August 1989.

Bernhardt, Sarah. *The Art of the Theatre.* New York: Books for Libraries Press, 1969.

Bernhardt, Sarah. *Memories of My Life.* New York: D. Appleton, 1907.

Izard, Forrest. *Sarah Bernhardt, An Appreciation.* New York: Sturgis & Walton Company,1915.

*New Theatre Quarterly,* Cambridge, MA, February 1994.

Skinner, Cornelia Otis. *Madame Sarah.* Boston: Houghton Mifflin Company, 1967.

*Smithsonian,* New York, August 2001.

*The Theatre Magazine,* Columbus, OH, 1906.

*Theatre Research International,* Cambridge, MA, Spring 1993.

*The Wave,* San Francisco, May 2, 1891.

# Leslie Carter

## Newspapers

*Argonaut,* San Francisco, August 4, 1897.

*New York Times,* November 14, 1937.

*San Francisco Call,* February 10, 1889.

*San Francisco Chronicle,* December 7, 1902.

*San Francisco Chronicle,* June 14, 1904.

## Books/Magazines/Historical Quarterlies

Belasco, David. *The Theatre Through Its Stage Door,* New York: Harper and Brothers Publishers, 1919.

*Liberty,* Silver Springs, MD, January 15, 1927–March 19, 1927.

*Sunset,* Tampa, FL, July 1904.

Timberlake, Craig. *The Bishop of Broadway, The Life and Work of David Belasco.* New York: Library Publishers Inc., 1954.

# Caroline Chapman

## Newspapers

*Daily Alta California,* San Francisco, May 24, 1853.

*Daily Alta California,* San Francisco, June 10, 1853.

*Daily Alta California,* San Francisco, June 29, 1853.

*Daily Alta California,* San Francisco, December 7, 1853.

*Daily Alta California,* San Francisco, January 1, 1862.

*Daily Alta California,* San Francisco, May 9, 1876.

*Daily Alta California,* San Francisco, May 13, 1876.

*Daily Alta California,* San Francisco, March 3, 1880.

*Gold Hill News,* Gold Hill, Nevada, May 15, 1865.

*Gold Hill News,* Gold Hill, Nevada, September 28, 1865.

*Gold Hill News,* Gold Hill, Nevada, April 6, 1871.

*San Francisco Call,* November 30, 1862.

*San Francisco Call,* October 10, 1887.

*San Francisco Call,* December 5, 1887.

*San Francisco Examiner,* July 16, 1928.

*San Francisco Herald,* June 20, 1854.

*San Francisco Herald,* March 27, 1857.

*San Francisco Herald,* April 3, 1859.

## Books/Magazines/Historical Quarterlies
Alley, B. F. *A History of Tuolumne County,* California Sonora, CA. Tuolumne Historical Society 1882.

# Charlotte Cushman
## Newspapers
*Berkeley Daily Gazette,* Berkeley, CA, September 17, 1907.

*Boston Morning Post,* April 8, 1837.

*Boston Morning Post,* October 19, 1841.

*The Boston Sunday Post,* April 13, 1913.

*Defiance Daily Crescent News,* Defiance, OH, February 23, 1912.

*The English Gentlemen,* London, May 16, 1846.

*The Fort Wayne News,* Fort Wayne, IN, December 1, 1899.

*Indiana County Gazette,* Indiana, PA, October 25, 1899.

*Iowa City Press,* Iowa City, IA, February 22, 1923.

*The Janesville Gazette,* Janesville, WI, February 21, 1876.

*Sacramento Daily Union,* February 3, 1855.

## Books/Magazines/Historical Quarterlies
Stebbins, Emma Charlotte Cushman. *Her Letters and Memoires of Her Life.* Cambridge, MA: The Riverside Press, 1878.

# Jeanne Eagels
## Newspapers
*The Capital Times,* Madison, WI, October 7, 1929.

*Hamilton Journal,* Hamilton, OH, January 3, 1925.

*The Kansas City Star,* Kansas City, MO, November 2, 1923.

*The Lawrence Daily Journal-World,* Lawrence, KS, March 28, 1931.

*The Lima News and Times-Democrat,* Lima, OH, July 1922.

*The New York Times,* December 27, 1926.

*The Newark Daily Advocate,* Newark, NJ, January 23, 1917.

*Oakland Tribune,* Oakland, CA, October 7, 1929.

*The Ogden Standard-Examiner,* Ogden City, UT, December 23, 1923.

*The Ogden Standard-Examiner,* Ogden City, UT, October 4, 1929.

*The Register,* Sandusky, OH, July 17, 1921.

*San Antonio Light,* San Antonio, TX, May 6, 1928.

*The Sheboygan Press,* Sheboygan, WI, October 4, 1929.

*Syracuse Herald,* Syracuse, NY, October 20, 1929.

*Thomasville Times-Enterprise,* Thomasville, GA, October 7, 1929.

*The Titusville Herald,* Titusville, PA, October 4, 1929.

*Wichita Daily Times,* Wichita Falls, TX, October 5, 1929.

## Books/Magazines/Historical Quarterlies

Doherty, Edward. *The Rain Girl: The Tragic Story of Jeanne Eagels.*
Philadelphia: Macrae-Smith Philadelphia, 1930.

# Catherine Hayes

## Newspapers

*Burlington Daily Hawk Eye,* Burlington, IA, October 22, 1857.

*Madison Daily Banner,* Madison, WI, January 10, 1853.

*Illustrated Times,* London, Middlesex, August 17, 1861.

## Books/Magazines/Historical Quarterlies

Ahlquist, Karen. *Democracy at the Opera.* New York: New York Press,
1997.

O'Mara, Joseph. *If These Walls Could Talk.* Limerick, Ireland: Limerick
Press Limerick,1972.

Preston, Katherine K. *Opera on the Road: Traveling Troupes in the U.S.,
1825–1860.* Champaign: University of Illinois Press, 1995.

Van der Pas, Peter W. *Kate Hayes.* Nevada County Historical Society
Bulletin, Vol. 42, No. I, January 1988.

Walsh, Basil. *Catherine Hayes: The Hibernian Prima Donna.* Dublin,
Ireland and Portland, OR: Irish Academic Press, 2000.

# Matilda Heron
## Books/Magazines/Historical Quarterlies
Browne, Ross J. *Review of Miss Heron's Performance.* Virginia City, NV: Enterprise, April 17, 1866.

Johnson, Allen and Malone Dumas. *Dictionary of American Biography.* New York: Charles Scribner's Sons, 1931.

*California Chronicle,* San Francisco, January 1854.

Wilson, James G. and John Fiske. *Encyclopedia of America Biography.* New York: D. Appleton, 1888.

# Laura Keene
## Newspapers
*Boston Post,* December 1, 1853.

*Boston Post,* March 11, 1859.

*Boston Daily Globe,* November 10, 1873.

*Decatur Republican,* Decatur, IL, November 13, 1873.

*Guernsey Jeffersonian,* Cambridge, OH, April 28, 1865.

*London Lady's Newspaper and Pictorial,* London, November 8, 1851.

*Logansport Pharos Tribune,* Logansport, IN, April 5, 1897.

*New York Daily Times,* February 23, 1856.

*The Wisconsin State Journal,* Madison, April 17, 1933.

## Books/Magazines/Historical Quarterlies
Bryan, Vernanne. *Laura Keene: A British Actress on the American Stage, 1826–1873.* Jefferson, NC and London: McFarland & Company, Inc., 1993.

# Adah Menken
## Newspapers
*The Edinburgh Evening Courant,* England, August 12, 1868.

*Lloyd's Weekly London Newspaper,* September 13, 1868.

## Books/Magazines/Historical Quarterlies

Davis, Sam. "The History of Nevada," *Nevada Monthly,* Vol. 2, July 1880.

Goose, Edmund. "The Life of Algernon Charles Swinburne," *Dictionary of National Biography,* Kessinger Publishing, 1917.

James, Edwin. *Biography of Adah Isaacs Menken.* New York: New York Press, 1881.

Mankowitz, Wolf Mazeppa. *The Lives, Loves, and Legends of Adah Isaacs Menken.* New York: Stein and Day Publishers, 1982.

Stoddard, Charles W. "La Belle Menken" *National Magazine,* February 1905.

# Helena Modjeska

## Newspapers

*Daily Alta California,* San Francisco, August 21, 1877.

*Daily Alta California,* San Francisco, August 26, 1877.

*Daily Nevada State Journal,* Reno, NV, October 31, 1877.

*Idaho Statesman,* Boise, ID, March 21, 1901.

*Idaho Statesman,* Boise, ID, March 22, 1901.

*Reno Evening Gazette,* Reno, NV, October 25, 1877.

*Reno Evening Gazette,* Reno, NV, October 29, 1877.

*San Francisco Call,* February 10, 1889.

*San Francisco Call,* January 21, 1906.

*San Francisco Call,* April 9, 1909.

*Territorial Enterprise,* Virginia City, NV, October 23, 1877.

## Books/Magazines/Historical Quarterlies

*Footlight,* Los Angeles, October 23–26, 1877.

Gronowicz, Antoni, *Modjeska, Her Life and Loves.* New York: Thomas Yoseloff, Inc., 1956.

Modjeska, Helena. *Memories and Impressions.* New York: MacMillan Publishing , 1910.

Payne, Theodore. *Life on the Modjeska Ranch in the Gay Nineties.* Los Angeles: The Kruckeberg Press, 1962.

Wingate, Charles E. *Shakespeare's Heroines on the Stage.* New York: Thomas Y. Crowell & Company, 1895.

# Catherine Norton Sinclair

## Newspapers

*Boston Morning Post*, August 19, 1837.

*Daily Banner, Cleveland*, OH, May 8, 1849.

*The Fort Wayne Times*, Fort Wayne, IN, February 19, 1852.

*Hawarden Independent*, Hawarden, IA, April 4, 1889.

*Independent American*, Platteville, WI, June 4, 1852.

*New York Daily Times*, January 26, 1852.

## Books/Magazines/Historical Quarterlies

Norton Sinclair Forrest, Catherine. *Testimony in the Forrest Divorce Case.* Philadelphia: Forgotten Books, 1850.

# Lillian Russell

## Newspapers

*Anaconda Standard*, Anaconda, MT, May 26, 1907.

*Anaconda Standard*, Anaconda, MT, May 29, 1907.

*Anaconda Standard*, Anaconda, MT, May 12, 1909.

*Argonaut*, Los Angeles, April 23, 1881.

*Argonaut*, Los Angeles, April 30, 1881.

*Argonaut*, Los Angeles, May 9, 1907.

*Argonaut*, Los Angeles, May 12, 1909.

*Montana Standard*, Butte, MT, May 7, 1978.

*Oneonta Daily Star*, Oneonta, NY, June 7, 1922.

*San Francisco Call*, April 8, 1881.

*San Francisco Call*, April 15, 1881.

*San Francisco Call*, April 27, 1881.

*San Francisco Call*, May 22, 1881.

## Books/Magazines/Historical Quarterlies

Auster, Albert. *Actress and Suffragist*. New York: Praeger Publisher, 1984.

Burke, John. *Duet in Diamonds: The Flamboyant Saga of Lillian Russell and Diamond Jim Brady in America's Gilded Age*. New York: GP Putnam's Sons, 1972.

*Cosmopolitan*, Harlan, IA, February–September 1922.

*Montana Standard*, Butte, MT, May 7, 1978.

*The Theatre Magazine*, New York, February 1905.

# Index

# About the Author

**Chris Enss** is a *New York Times* bestselling author who has been writing about women of the Old West for more than a dozen years. She has penned more than thirty published books on the subject. Her book entitled *Object Matrimony: The Risky Business of Mail Order Matchmaking* on the Western Frontier won the Elmer Kelton Award for best non-fiction book of 2013. Enss's book *Sam Sixkiller: Frontier Cherokee Lawman* was named Outstanding Book on Oklahoma History by the Oklahoma Historical Society. She received the Spirit of the West Alive award, cosponsored by the *Wild West Gazette*, celebrating her efforts to keep the spirit of the Old West alive for future generations